A Purpose f

Sir John Glubb

A Purpose for Living

LONDON
SPCK

First published 1980
SPCK
Holy Trinity Church
Marylebone Road
London NW1 4SU

Filmset in Great Britain by
Northumberland Press Ltd, Gateshead, Tyne and Wear
Printed by
Fletcher and Son Ltd, Norwich

ISBN 0 281 03720 5

Contents

Introduction

It seems to me that, deeply embedded in our human nature, there is a profound desire to feel that we are useful, that we are wanted, that we are doing a good job of work. At a more superficial level of our minds, we may think that we want to enjoy ourselves, to have fun, to live in luxury and pleasure. But the excitement to be derived from living a gay life soon palls as we advance in years. More and more, we begin to ask ourselves what is the good of it all.

Of course our circumstances vary. Those who are happily married and have a family can find therein a justification for their lives. Those who are so fortunate as to love their work can find satisfaction in their absorption in it, and in the increase of their own skill. But both these forms of achieving a satisfying life seem today in the Western world to be on the decrease. The frequency of divorce or of promiscuity renders happy family life increasingly difficult. The reduction in craftmanship as against dull, monotonous, dehumanized work makes it more and more exceptional for men to find joy and fulfilment in their work. Starved of human love and of interest in our work, we ask wearily what is the object of our lives. Looked at in such an atmosphere, life seems indeed to be aimless and futile.

But if we could see an object to live for, if we formed part of a mighty army marching to a glorious victory and eternal peace under a deeply loved Commander, all this would be changed. Shoulder to shoulder with our comrades, inspired by the joy of serving a great and noble cause, devoted to our beloved Chief, we should swing through life full of happiness and devotion. Is this just a silly dream? Personally I do not think so.

Some fortunate people who have discovered useful ways of service are able, even if only weakly and partially, to taste such joys. But the majority of the human race fail to find the happiness and the fulfilment of their instinctive wish to be useful. The only way we can imagine in which the whole human race could find the deep joy of fulfilment through service would be if they discovered the secret of service to God. If God is the Creator of the whole world, then his servants would be freed from hatred, jealousy, arrogance and small-mindedness, for all would be marching in the ranks of the same army.

A profound and bitter cynicism has permeated the civilization of the West. Belief in God is too often greeted with a sneer. We allow ourselves to be deterred too easily by such contemptuous remarks from devoting any thought to the existence of God. Yet it cannot possibly be denied that if he does exist the whole of life is transformed. Think of it seriously for a moment. If God really exists, if he knows *me* and loves me, the whole of life is filled with purpose. If God exists, only he is of any importance.

In this book, I have tried firstly to consider, purely by the light of reason, whether God exists or not. I must say that it seems to me that reason, neglecting all claims to authority, indicates that the odds are heavily in favour of his existence. This may not constitute mathematical proof, but I cannot think of any alternative theory which accounts for the human situation. Assuming then that he does exist, I have attempted to consider certain aspects of the life of Christ, as illustrating the nature of God. Finally I have tried to show how I think that belief in the existence of God can affect our modern world.

I do not claim to possess any special qualifications for the task. I do not wish to quote authority or to claim any for myself. I am not clever or intellectual. I am just an ordinary, average man. But the great majority of the human race are ordinary, average people like me. This is my excuse for venturing into a field on which I am so ill qualified to speak. My thoughts are doubtless often too earth-bound and will frequently be erroneous. But I do not offer them as teaching, but as notes made during my journey through life, which I hope may be of interest to some at least of my fellow travellers.

I do not visualize this book as one to be read through once and for all and returned to the library. It consists of thoughts, and comments on various aspects and experiences of human living. It is intended rather to be a book of reference to be picked up at odd moments, when the various ideas which I have formed in the course of my life can be considered at leisure. If it can bring comfort or encouragement to any of my fellow-pilgrims, I shall be thankful to my Creator and my Saviour.

1 *How Small We Are*

Someone has said that the trouble with man is not so much his wickedness as his smallness. It might perhaps have been expected that an age which has learned so much about the vast distances of space, and the utter insignificance of the planet on which we live, might have increasingly realized our own lack of importance. Tiny and ephemeral insects on an unimportant speck of dust floating in apparently endless space, we might have acquired a modicum of realism sufficient, at least partly, to appreciate our own nothingness.

Yet, in fact, we cannot avoid the conclusion that never before has man been so cocksure, so impertinent, and so laughably arrogant. It is difficult to find words in the English language to describe the rank absurdity of our antics. The universe, we are told, is thousands of millions of years old; we live only for sixty or seventy years. Space seems to go on forever, but we can think only in terms of miles or kilometres.

The greatest scientists protest that the knowledge we possess, even of the physical working of the world about us, is negligible compared to the endless mysteries by which we are surrounded. And these limitations apply even to our material surroundings, which we can examine, see, handle and weigh. Regarding the more impalpable forces which everywhere envelop us, we know virtually nothing at all. Even our own mental processes are beyond our understanding, not to speak of our emotions. Who can assess the effects of influence, spreading in ever widening circles around every human being? The inspiration of the artist, the poet and the musician are beyond our powers of analysis. Yet these mysteries involve ourselves alone. If we knew anything at all, surely we should know ourselves before anything else. The powers we possess to communicate with one another without the use of speech or hearing, and the processes of intuition are still a mystery to us.

We live in time, and indeed our lives are obsessed by it. We all carry watches, we are surrounded by clocks, we speak constantly of saving time. We want cars which go faster, and have more acceleration to enable us to overtake and pass others. But when we reach our destination, we often have nothing to do but read a newspaper. Or is our craving for speed due to the nervous restlessness of our unsatisfied souls?

Time is measured for us by the alternation of day and night, by summer and winter, or by the passage of our own lives. We are haunted by fear of the swift passing of the years, by the advent of old age, the loss of youthful powers and pleasures, and the approach of death. Time dominates our brief ephemeral lives. Yet time is also an incomprehensible mystery. When did time begin? What happened before time began? Will time end? If so, what will happen then? If time never began and will never end, we are living in eternity. But eternity is incomprehensible to the human mind. This is not a question of being right or wrong in our views. Eternity just cannot be grasped by our minds.

'I don't believe in God,' a young woman said to me recently. 'Before long science will have discovered everything.' This is an interesting form of narrow thought, for 'discovering' means to find out facts hitherto unknown to us, but which have always existed. If we discover more of them, we have merely reduced our own ignorance. Yet when we discover some new aspect of creation, we are as proud as if we had created it ourselves. Thus if we make new discoveries of the working of the material world, we shall not have solved any of our fundamental problems.

We shall not have learned the origins of the universe, or the reason for its creation. We shall not have discovered the Creator, and, as a result, we shall not have come to understand the object of our own existence. Yet, if we are to lead meaningful lives, we must above all ascertain why we are here, and why we were created, so that we can render worthwhile service to our Creator, and can devote our brief lives to the furtherance of his plans.

People perhaps once thought that the thunder was the roaring of an angry god. Now we know it is an electrical discharge. But we are no nearer finding out the object and meaning of our lives. Our discovery of certain material facts of the universe have intoxicated our little minds. Like impudent cock-sparrows, we hop around chirping our elation at our own cleverness, and our defiance of the Creator of that universe of which we have explored a tiny fraction of the margin, but of the reason for the existence of which we have not the vaguest conception.

But the smallness of our minds is not limited to our arrogant defiance of Infinity and Eternity. The greater part of our thoughts all day long is devoted to our personal affairs and our petty rivalries. Most of our thoughts are concerned only with ourselves. We seek to enlarge our importance by endless criticism of everyone else, whether we express our judgements aloud, or brood over them in our own minds.

> Why has one of our colleagues been promoted? He does not know much of his job. It seems like sheer favouritism.
>
> Mrs Jones on the Committee annoys me so much. She always likes to hear her own voice and will not let anyone else speak.
>
> Why should the manager be getting three times my salary? It is true he is thirty years older than I am, but that only proves that he must be out of date.

Why should we co-operate with Europe? I just hate the French and the Germans.

But perhaps we are not all spiteful—at least not all the time. Some of us enjoy our work and are interested to see it grow. Others only yawn through their office hours, but derive their principal pleasure playing bridge every evening. To others, watching football is their hobby, or looking forward to the next drink. The catalogue of our interests, our passions or our jealousies could be endlessly prolonged. Some of our pastimes are innocent, but are they worth the devotion of a lifetime? Some of our activities are distorted by spite or jealousy. Many of us derive comfort from saving money. An increasing bank balance does lend a certain feeling of security, until suddenly we are assailed by an incurable disease or crippled in a car accident, and money loses all its interest for us.

The unending succession of events, of work and pleasure, of joy, disaster or depression, fills all our thoughts. Some of our activities are harmless, some are directed to injure others, some to help those in need. The point which impresses me, however, is that we have only one life to live. When we reach its close, will we be satisfied with the thought that we have spent it accumulating money, which ceases to have any importance for us as our end approaches? Or that we have passed our happiest hours playing bridge, tennis or darts?

As far as we know, we shall not live again on this earth. This was our one opportunity. Now that it is nearing its end, can we congratulate ourselves that we have done everything possible to make a really worthwhile contribution? What contribution could we have made? To make a contribution suggests that there is a cause to be served. Is the attempt to help our neighbours or to relieve the unfortunate a worthwhile cause to which to devote our lives? Many of them will be ungrateful, will repay us with unkindness, or will speak evil of us. But even those who repay our kindness with affection will soon, like ourselves, be dead.

✠

When we ask if our lives were worthwhile, we are opening a new world of thought. Our materialistic world is increasingly governed by figures, that is to say by quantity. Our gross national product is the quantity of articles which we make. We do not attempt to record their quality. Sixty or seventy years ago, we prided ourselves rightly that British goods were always of good workmanship, high quality and durability. Now such standards have long been abandoned. Even in our material dealings, quality has given place to quantity.

We boast of the increasing numbers of young people who now attend universities, but we do not bother to inquire into the academic standards of the graduates, far less their moral characters. All through our thinking quantity has replaced quality. Yet, in ordinary conversation, we still retain the words 'good' and 'worthwhile' without appreciating that, in so doing, we open the door into the moral world. If men were only animals, if the material objects around us, which we can see and touch, were the only things which exist, there would be no such phenomenon as goodness, no life which we could call worthwhile.

We do not expect a well-nurtured domestic dog to share his dinner with a hungry stray. As far as we can see, his outlook is 'practical'—he wishes to get all he can for himself. But when Mother Teresa of Calcutta gives up all her life to serve the starving and the dying, we cannot but exclaim in admiration. Without thinking very clearly about the issues involved, we pay spontaneous tribute to such goodness. But should we admire such a life, if this world is all that exists? If the only object of our lives is to get through them with as little discomfort as possible and then cease to live, Mother Teresa is just a fool. She would have been more sensible to go into business and make enough money to live in a comfortable house and drive a large car.

If we express our admiration for devotion, compassion and self-sacrifice, we are, consciously or unconsciously, admitting that there *are* other things than the material objects which surround us. But if we are merely animals, how did such ideas ever enter our minds? If we are just the result of millions of years of physical evolution, why are we filled with admiration for spiritual qualities, resulting in the voluntary abandonment of material objects of desire? For evolution is the survival of the fittest, the result of successful competition against others.

The only answer to this question seems to me to be that there must be something in human nature which is completely other than the struggle for physical survival and material success. We are obliged to assume that some other element lies hidden in our complex human nature, which does not accept the survival of the fittest as its code of life. An element, indeed, which totally rejects the theory that life is merely a struggle for survival which ends in death.

This other factor in our make-up tends indeed to be ashamed of the idea that life is a process of grab—a battle to defeat or outwit other human beings in the struggle for material wealth. This mysterious element in our mentality wishes to give up its material supports and devote itself to service and self-sacrifice. It feels strongly that it is more blessed to give than to receive.

Most of us compromise between these two conflicting

instincts in our mentality. We spend most of our time in our daily routine, trying to make money or to surround ourselves with more physical comforts or amenities. But the other element within us periodically asserts itself. We are a little ashamed of thinking *only* of ourselves. So we subscribe to a charity, assist an indigent relative, or give our services in some local church or social activity. Such a subterfuge is no more than a bribe to quieten the inner voice, which tells us that money and pleasure are not really the objects to which we should devote the only life on earth which we seem likely to live.

Such methods cannot ultimately succeed in stifling the inner voice which tells us that we are not fulfilling our obligations and that our lives should be dedicated to something better. We may grow materially richer, but we are not at ease. For that inner voice is uncompromising. It keeps whispering that the only way to real peace is complete dedication to service, regardless of our private desires or financial anxieties. Our souls are restless and unhappy, but we struggle to stifle their voices. Business activities, an improving bank balance, smarter clothes, a feeling of social superiority, hobbies, pleasure, alcohol or drugs assist us to forget the still small voice—at least for most of the time. Perhaps we even rise to a position of authority, and have under us subordinates who obey our orders. This swells our feeling of importance, and causes us a good deal of self-satisfaction.

But sooner or later the end draws near. We have but a short time to live. The money, the fame, the honours and the importance are suddenly valueless and insipid. We look back on an active life of work and pleasure, on our battles with rivals, our little meannesses, and our insensibility to those who needed the help which we were in a position to give. All is over now. The account will soon be closed. All has been shown to us too late to have been nothing but vanity and vexation of spirit.

2 *Theories*

The superficial life described in the previous chapter—engrossed in day to day pleasures or worries—cannot be said to be satisfying. At this stage of our argument, we come to a parting of the ways. If we wish, we may decide that this life is indeed unsatisfactory, but that this is the way life is. We are born without our consent and we are obliged to get through as best we can. To induce cheerfulness and forget the futility of it all, the best remedy is alcohol. We are the innocent victims of blind chance, which brought the world and ourselves into existence. If our lot in life becomes unbearable, we can end it ourselves. It does indeed appear that societies where belief in God is weakest often have the highest suicide rates.

Persons who profess to believe that there is no object in life tend to be cynical and unhappy. We cannot avoid wishing to play a significant role in a great and benevolent plan. Deprived of this possibility, we spread discouragement and bitterness around us. Unless something can penetrate the defensive armour of such people and touch the sensitive spark of love which lies buried in every human soul—unless this occurs, they die in bitterness and despair.

But all this unhappiness is unnecessary. The facts of human life do not justify so gloomy an attitude. Those who have sometimes heard that still small voice, or those who are weary of the imbecilities, the frivolities and the heartbreak of life, will wish to explore further.

The point which caught our attention in the previous chapter was precisely that small voice within us, which seems to tell us that the survival of the fittest is not the object of human existence. We sense something within us which tells us that giving is better than grabbing.

It does not seem credible that a mechanical universe, solely controlled by chance, or the physical competition of evolution, could give birth in us to a feeling that we ought to be giving not getting. Such a feeling seems to be totally opposed to the ruthless struggles of natural life, which we see about us. It seems as if this quality in the human race must have some other source than chance or the evolutionary struggle for survival. Where *can* this strange element have come from, seeming, as it does, to be totally opposed to the trend of the material world?

The greater part of the progress of natural science has been achieved by the formulation of theories. The scientist conceives an idea of what might be the cause of the phenomenon which confronts him. Having drawn up his theory, he and his colleagues carry out as many experiments as possible to test its correctness. If any of the experiments disprove the theory, he will be obliged to abandon it or modify it, and to start again. If, however, all the experiments appear to confirm the theory, it may in due course be recognized as a law.

The theories which I propose to submit to the reader are the result of the experience of a lifetime. The conclusions are my own. I do not claim for them any authority or dogma, and the reader is free to agree with them or to reject them. I believe that the human mind is so small in comparison with God that any ideas we may formulate are certain to be narrow and limited and in many directions completely erroneous, like the impressions of the world formed in the mind of a baby a year old.

It seems to me that God himself has imposed these limitations on our intellects in accordance with his plans for our development, as will be discussed in a later chapter. I only offer humbly these thoughts to my fellow human beings, because they have helped me, and may also, I hope, be of assistance to my contemporaries.

✠

These then are the theories which have evolved in my mind in the course of a long life. Firstly, I do not believe that the world, as we see it all around us, has developed from pure chance, without any mind to invent or to guide it. It is easy to say that the universe began with a cosmic explosion, but this speculation, whether or not it be correct, only takes us one step further back. There must have been something there to explode, and how did that something come into existence? Or if the explosion occurred before anything existed, then it must have been a pure act of creation. In any case, the universe seems to extend into infinity in both space and time, and these are conceptions which cannot be grasped by the human brain. Consequently, the claim that the science produced by our human intelligences will soon 'know everything' seems to me unlikely of fulfilment. Thus my first theory is that there must have been a Creator.

Secondly, I should like to refer to the mystery of life. We can examine and classify the earth's rocks, its minerals and its gases. But how were these transformed into living plants, and subsequently into self-propelled animals, birds and fishes. The creation of life remains a mystery, which may suggest to us the intervention of some outside but invisible agency. My second theory, therefore, is that the mystery of the appearance of life presupposes the existence of a supreme intellect, which planned and directed these phenomena.

Thirdly, having noted the unexplained mysteries of creation and of life, we come to evolution, or the changes which life has undergone. Here, perhaps, we may intervene with a confident smile. 'That is something', we say, 'which we *can* understand. Evolution is the answer. No intervention of God is necessary. It all just happens automatically.' In this respect, our self-assurance seems to be largely due to primitive ideas of religion. It was once thought that, if God intervened, he would do so in visible form, with flashes of lightning, roaring winds, legions of angels or chariots of fire. If we cannot see visible signs from heaven, we assume that God has not played any part in the changes in the world. In a later chapter, we will discuss what seem to be the reasons for the fact that God's interventions in the world are almost always invisible. For the moment, we will limit ourselves to the suggestion that divine intervention is not necessarily visible.

If, however, God bestowed life on plants and animals, he seems to have endowed them with the capability of adapting themselves to their surroundings. If it is necessary to his 'policy' to remain invisible, then the only course he could adopt would be to endow all living things with a built-in capability to adapt themselves.

Some people say that we know how all the processes of nature work, and that there is no need for God any more. This does not explain who created nature to work so smoothly. It is absurd to suggest that God ought to have made the world in such a way that his intervention would be necessary in a miracle to make (let us say) animals with heavy coats shed their fur, if they moved to a warmer area. The fact that animals adapt themselves to living conditions is an additional proof of the wonder of creation.

I have already referred to the fact that God's miracles were once believed to be necessarily visible. Our Lord himself was asked to prove the validity of his mission by giving a visible sign. He refused to call down fire from heaven, and his opponents consequently denounced him as an impostor. But he himself gave us the explanation—'The kingdom of God', he said, 'is within you.' There is a small voice which tells us that there is within us something which cannot be accounted for by evolution. It is this something which urges us not to seek only our personal advantage or to trample upon those who oppose us.

Personally I cannot think of any explanation for this persistent feeling implanted in our deepest mentality other than the belief that God, at some stage in our development, added this element to our perhaps originally animal nature. But there is not the slightest doubt that this little bit of heaven is deeply embedded in our human make-up, and that it cannot be attributed to automatic evolutionary causes or to blind chance.

Some may reply that conscience is purely the result of education. Our parents, they say, told us that we should be polite and unselfish, and the memories of these exhortations occasionally return to us in after life. I do not think that this explanation is supported by facts. There are many recorded cases of professional criminals, brought up in desperately vicious surroundings, and taught by their elders to steal, who have been suddenly converted. Something has touched the divine spark within them. With tears of joy and penitence, they have been converted and have consecrated the rest of their lives to service, some even taking holy orders and becoming ordained ministers of religion. Such persons are often more dedicated than those brought up in more respectable surroundings, whose parents and teachers did indeed inculcate into their minds the need for politeness and unselfishness.

I have indeed encountered something of the kind in my own limited experience. For many years I was in intimate contact with some of the more primitive Arab tribes.

These men were simple and unsophisticated, but they were proud of their martial valour. Raiding and plunder were the occupations which chiefly attracted them, and they felt no compunction about killing men, whether in battle or in the pursuit of family blood feuds. I enlisted many such men for public security duties.

Now and again, I would collect a party of these men and explain to them that it was our duty to devote our lives to service, not to plunder or self-interest. Not only were we under an obligation to serve, but also to raise the standard of morals among the people by the example we set them. As government servants, men and women would look at us and be influenced by us. The whole moral standard of the nation could be raised by the example of our dedicated lives. No one would have accused these men of effeminacy, yet I have often seen them so affected by this talk of dedication to service that the tears actually rolled down their weather-beaten cheeks to their beards. Men whose lives had previously been devoted to killing and plunder were so transformed that their moral example did indeed effect the virtual disappearance of crime in the area. In official religion they were not Christians but Muslims. Yet, within their souls slept the divine spark which, when fanned, was capable of transforming all their lives.

The fourth theory which I wish to submit is that, at a certain stage, God decided to raise the level of his creation by the introduction of Man. It is, perhaps, interesting to note that the first chapter of Genesis depicts God as saying, 'Let us make man in our image, after our likeness'. It is specifically stated that man was made after the fishes, the birds, the animals and the reptiles. Perhaps some already existent form of animal life was used for the purpose, perhaps not. But this new species was to be in the image of God. This obviously does not refer to his physical appearance, for God is a spirit. But man was to resemble God in that he was to have within him a spark of the divine Spirit.

I do not wish to quote Genesis in an authoritarian manner, or to state dogmatically that this statement must be believed. But all through the Old Testament—and indeed all through the recorded history of the human race—men and women have now and again received flashes of intuition, which have later proved to be correct. It seems to me that this passage in Genesis may very possibly be something of the kind.

The theories which I wish to put forward are, therefore the following:

1. That the universe was created by God.
2. That the appearance of life on earth must be attributed to God.
3. That evolution is a system installed by God to enable living things to adjust.
4. That man has within him a seed of the divine Spirit which is God.

3 *What is Man?*

Of what does man consist, and why, we may ask, did God create him? We have reached the conclusion so far that man may well have been of animal origin, but that God implanted in him a spark of his own divinity. The presence of this spark enabled God to communicate directly with man.

Our minds are so limited that we cannot understand God. Nevertheless we have to live our lives, however insignificant, and it seems to me to be incumbent on us to use what brains we have to try to understand.

It appears to me reasonable to suppose that God does indeed feel an affection for us as his creatures, and that he wishes to raise us to a higher moral status. Only so can we grow nearer to him and be able to learn to communicate with him and to understand his wishes.

At this stage, we meet with the problem of what we mean by morals, a question involving the whole essence of man. As far as we know, animals do not consider the laws of morality. A cat catching a mouse does not pause to consider whether the action is right or wrong. Here then we find another characteristic of man—that he is convinced that some actions are right and some are wrong. He may sometimes deliberately choose to do wrong, because it gives him immediate gratification, or because he has been told that everyone does such things nowadays. In spite of this, however, he is sure that right and wrong exist. He may steal, let us say, and soothe his conscience by claiming that society has denied him justice. But his rebellion against society assumes that the community has behaved 'wrongly' towards him. He may himself consider that it would be wrong to defraud his fellow thieves. Thus the fact that man is acutely conscious of right and wrong further proves that he is not just an animal.

Once again, it is impossible to assume that the sense of right and wrong is the result of evolution. Some might claim that the feeling of a duty to do right is due to the 'herd instinct', or to the desire to preserve the solidarity of the group. But in fact we find that this moral sense has constantly led to the disruption of the community. All through history, we find people denouncing the wrongs of society in which they live. Often they have faced intense unpopularity, and even martyrdom, at the hands of their own herd. We cannot therefore avoid the conclusion that the sense of right and wrong is a quality implanted in the human race by a Power outside ourselves, in accordance with a policy intended to raise the status of man to communion with God. It is worthy of note that our Lord —sometimes mistakenly depicted as meek and mild—was sternly realistic in this respect. He announced that he had come to the earth not to bring peace but a sword. The emergence from animality to divine communion would require many a stern struggle.

When considering the essential composition of man, we must also include the capability which we possess to look at ourselves, so to speak, from the outside. As far as we can judge, animals are not able to look at and examine their own conduct.

The theory which we are considering is that God has planted a divine element in man, to enable him to achieve a moral status which will enable him to communicate with God himself. If God were, by a wave of his wand, to make man 'good', the transformation would not involve any moral advance in the human race. It would not produce personalities, but mere puppets. We can easily understand that such moral advance can be achieved only by effort on the part of man himself. In order to lead him to make such an effort, the power of self-examination of his own conduct would obviously be essential. This faculty was, therefore, bestowed on him by God, to give him the incentive to embark on the struggle for self-improvement. Man's capacity to examine the morality of his own actions would not have assisted him in the survival of the fittest, nor can we see any way in which physical evolution could produce in him the ability to examine his own moral conduct.

Another interesting aspect of the subject of morality is the fact that men, of every race and religion of which I have heard, universally suffer under a feeling of guilt. When I used to sit on the ground with a circle of Arab desert tribesmen, one or other of them would now and again heave a deep sigh and murmur audibly, 'I ask pardon of God for my great guilt'.

If men are only animals and all we have to do is to grab as many material objects as we can and then die, why do all men feel a conviction that they have fallen short of their duty? To me the most reasonable solution of the mystery of our feelings of guilt is that this also is the result of that divine instinct implanted in our souls, to draw us nearer to God. 'Our hearts are restless till they rest in Thee,' said St Augustine of Hippo. No truer word was ever spoken. Our hearts are restless until we find God, and thereby a worthy purpose for the devotion of our lives.

It is perhaps also worth noticing that the eminent psychiatrist, Dr Jung, after spending a lifetime treating mental patients, came to the conclusion that lack of religious belief was one of the principal reasons for mental illness. Many of his patients only recovered their mental balance when they had acquired a convinced religious belief. In the words of Nicolas Berdyaev, 'Man without

God ceases to be man.' The conclusion seems to be that belief in the existence of God is an essential part of an integrated human personality. Our minds are restless and unbalanced until we find God, and thence a logical reason for living. Statistics reinforce this view by showing a constantly increasing number of mental patients in our hospitals, not to mention suicides and nervous breakdowns. These trends seem to increase in proportion as religious belief wanes, even in wealthy societies where there are scarcely any poor people.

It seems remarkable, to say the least, if God does not exist and material objects are the only reality, that belief in God should be so closely connected with human sanity. If, however, we accept the theory that man may originally have been an animal into whom God has inserted some spark of his own divinity, then it seems to be logical enough that the human race is now half-animal and half-spirit, and that this combination will not work smoothly in this life, unless both of its composing elements receive due consideration.

I sometimes used to wonder why people who did not believe were often so active in propagating their hostility to religion. For even if one does not believe in it, religion, as Edward Gibbon said, is valuable to the magistrate. In other words, it can reduce the crime rate. But it seems to me now that the violence of their opposition is itself a tribute to the vital part which religion plays in human nature, because its seed is planted in every human soul.

Mankind cannot live in internal harmony without a belief in God, yet the animal part of his make-up dreads it, because it constitutes a rival to his sensual nature. He sees himself torn between his carnal passions and between his longing for something spiritual, sublime and beautiful, above his animal instincts. So bitter is this struggle that some people would make every effort to destroy belief in God, even if it should lead to the collapse of society.

In 1789 the French revolutionaries declared the abolition of Christianity, but their efforts were unavailing. The Russian revolution has fought against belief in God for sixty years with all the resources of the state, yet religion is still alive and active in the Soviet empire. As St John says at the beginning of his Gospel, 'The light shines in the darkness, and the darkness has not been able to overcome it'. I believe the reason to be that human nature is half-body and half-spirit. Authoritarian prohibitions cannot stifle the longing in people's souls for the peace and splendour of the spiritual world.

If religion were but a foolish fancy, there would be no need to fight it so bitterly. It could be left either to survive or to fade out. It is because it is a matter of life and death deep down in every human soul, that it provokes such bitter hostility. Thus atheists themselves are witnesses to the deep roots of the Spirit in the human soul.

We may also include the faculty of speech as a divine gift, necessary to our instruction, co-operation, and moral progress. Moreover speech led to writing, although this was only achieved in historical times. Speech is, perhaps, less obviously a spiritual gift, than is a knowledge of right and wrong. Animals and birds whinny, chatter and sing to one another. Yet it may well be argued that speech was a necessity for the moral progress of man, permitting him to discuss such questions with his fellow human beings. Moreover speech seems to be essential to co-operation between members of the community, for, as we shall see later, love is the key to our moral progress. It is easier to love and to help our neighbours whom we can see, than to love God whom we cannot see.

The chief factor, however, which distinguishes man from the animals is his possession of Free Will—a subject which we shall discuss in our next chapter.

4 *Free Will*

The conception of man's freedom to act as he wishes is absolutely basic to the relationship between God and man. Actions carried out under the threat of fear or compulsion are of no moral value—a principle which it is absolutely vital for us to grasp.

Human beings endlessly criticize God for the present state of the world. Or alternatively they quote the present state of the world as proof that there cannot be a God, or that he is dead, or indifferent to what happens to the human race. If there really were a loving God, they say, he would surely put an end to wars, murder, violence and terrorism, and the many other crimes which cause so much human suffering. Such complaints bring out a number of points, which may be dealt with one by one.

Firstly, such grumbling suggests that only the present life is important. We have already pointed out in Chapter I that we are living in eternity. Our earthly lives are pathetically short and we look forward to more blessed states of existence hereafter. The fact that we are not always happy on earth is not, therefore, a major reason for criticizing God.

Secondly, the most basic foundation of all our relations with God is the fact that actions which we are forcibly obliged to perform possess no moral value. Moral merit can only be earned if we perform good deeds by our own volition.

Thirdly, what action do such grumblers wish God to take to prevent wars and violence? Should he take overt measures to ensure that soldiers, terrorists or statesmen who plan wars, should suddenly all fall dead or be struck down by lightning? If God were once to take such evident action, the whole human race would be cowed. Possibly official wars might cease, but men would live in constant fear of further divine action and would move stealthily about in abject terror.

If such a result were achieved, it would completely destroy the possibility of man achieving higher moral standards to enable him to draw nearer to God. Living in constant servile fear of divine punishment, he would be reduced to slavery. But the service of God, we are told, is perfect freedom, the only condition in which voluntary and loving service can be rendered.

It is for these reasons that we may take it as an axiom that *God never uses force*. Man, with his limited mental capacity, unconsciously visualizes God as a larger version of himself. When human governments meet with opposition, they readily use force to preserve their own authority. All through human history, men have expected God to mete out violent punishment to those who transgress his commandments. People constantly visualize God as being angry, or as desiring to revenge himself against those who oppose or criticize him. In so doing, human beings merely attribute their own mentality to God. This is what *they* would do under the circumstances. A basic fact which we must completely accept and continually remember is that *God, however he may be, is totally unlike man*. To attribute to God the thoughts and sentiments of men must therefore always be absurd.

Man may (or may not) be descended from an animal form, raised to a higher status by divine action. God is the Creator of all things, animate or inanimate. In his primitive state, man may have risen through physical struggle against his rivals, thereby acquiring a bellicose spirit of retaliation and revenge. But God is spirit, utterly different from human beings. Indeed he created every living thing. Men are his creatures, not his competitors. It is ridiculous to imagine that he could feel resentment against his own creatures. We may, therefore, immediately rule out suggestions that God can be in any way angry or vindictive against his creation. In considering his relations with human beings, we can only assume that he wishes to raise them to a moral level which will enable them to communicate with him.

We have already concluded that God wishes to raise men to a higher moral plane, and that actions performed out of fear possess no moral value. This conclusion refutes all suggestions that God should intervene to prevent wars, violence or crime. To raise man nearer to himself, he must allow him freedom of choice in his way of life. Only if he is free to choose wrong does man's choice of right possess any moral value, and give him the capability of rising gradually to a higher moral status.

The grant of this freedom of choice to man obviously allows him the opportunity to choose wrong. This may lead him to oppress and injure his fellow men and women or the animal creation, resulting in crime, violence, war, cruelty or dishonesty, which we blame God for permitting. We can now see clearly that the existence of evil, crime and violence is the result of God's grant of Free Will to men. For him to put a stop to crime and violence would reduce the whole human race to the status of puppets, with no freedom of choice in their actions. But if we rule out the possibility of God's direct intervention—so as not to destroy our freedom of choice—how is he to execute his desire to raise us to a higher moral level, so that we can communicate with him?

We are accustomed to communicate with one another by speech, or perhaps in writing or by the use of signs. If God does not use these human methods of communication, we assume that he is not influencing us or our society. But in fact there are already indications that men can communicate with one another without the use of speech or sight or even without physical propinquity. We may call this faculty thought-transference, extra-sensory perception or any other name. If human beings can thus communicate with one another, it would be absurd to claim that God is unable to do so. There would, therefore, seem to be strong reasons for believing that God can insert thoughts into our minds without using sound or sight. Moreover it would be essential that we should be unaware whence these thoughts come. For if we knew that they were an order from our Creator, the fact would constitute direct intervention, and fear would compel us to obey. Thus the element of doubt in our minds as to the source from which the thought comes, allows us to make our own free choice as to the course we will follow. This freedom, as we have seen, is essential if the choice we make is to possess moral value.

The beauty and subtlety of the system may well amaze us. By it, God can lead us gently and quietly to make choices which will raise our moral status, without our knowing for certain that it is really he who leads us to make such choices. If we knew positively that he was giving these orders our actions would be dictated by fear and we would therefore cease to be free and our conduct would consequently possess no moral value.

We may here pause to recollect that in the previous chapter we noted as one of God's gifts to man, his conviction of the existence of right and wrong, and his sense of guilt at his own unworthiness. Now that we have discovered the possibility that God speaks to us by extra-sensory perception, we may envisage the probability that our belief in the existence of right and wrong is inspired by God, although we do not know the source of our convictions. Similarly, awareness of our own guilt, which we call conscience, may well be infused into our minds in the same manner.

Another word which has often been used in religious writings during the last fifty or sixty years, is 'guidance'. The writers claim that, somehow or other, God guides their conduct, if they pause to ask his will, and on condition that they are absolutely prepared to obey. But we complain so endlessly of the state of the world and of the martyrdom of man, that we may consider in the next chapter how we ourselves would like our lives to be.

5 *The World of Heart's Desire*

Ah love, could thou and I with fate conspire
To wreck this sorry scheme of things entire,
Would we not shatter it to bits, and then
Remould it nearer to the heart's desire.

Thus sang the cynical Umar Khayyam, some eight hundred and seventy years ago. But let us take to ourselves the power which he had to admit regretfully that he did not possess. We too endlessly lament the troubles of our world and the sorry scheme of things entire, so let us remould the world as we would like it to be.

Perhaps the fact which gives rise to most of our complaints, at least when we are no longer young, is physical pain. Young people may at times suffer intense pain as the result of wounds or accidents, as also do young women in childbirth, but they suffer less from illness than do old people.

When we consider physical pain, the first point which strikes us is that it provides a necessary warning of danger. The sudden pain which we feel, when we touch a hot stove, causes us to snatch our hand away. If we felt no pain, we might leave it on the stove until all the flesh was burnt away. In the same way, pain warns us that we are suffering from appendicitis, and enables us to undergo the surgical operation which cures us in a few days. If we had not felt the pain, we should have neglected our condition until it ultimately resulted in death. Thus, at the very beginning of our inquiry into pain, we find that it is essential to our survival as a warning of danger. It is difficult to see how this problem could be avoided, unless our bodies were made immune to physical injury, a change so drastic as utterly to change all human life.

But pain also exercises the most fundamental influences on our lives in every direction. If we could not feel pain many forms of courage would cease to exist. When a man enters a burning home to rescue his wife and children, he is rightly hailed as a hero. But if fire did not hurt, there would be no courage involved. When a man in the forest fights a bear or a tiger to protect his family, it is the knowledge that he may suffer injuries causing acute pain, which constitutes the bravery of his action. When a party of soldiers bars the path to the enemy, in order to defend their country, their women and their children, it is the knowledge that they thereby risk agonising wounds, which constitutes the nobility of their action. 'Pain', writes Evelyn Underhill, 'and the willingness to risk pain, alone gives dignity and worth to human love and is the price of its creative power.'

Most of us will agree that self-sacrifice for the sake of other people is one of the characteristics which most excite our admiration. Indeed it is one of the chief qualities which distinguish men from animals, though it is true that animals can show such self-sacrifice. I remember seeing a herd of gazelles chased across the desert by men in a car. When the herd were nearly exhausted, an old buck turned back and stood defiantly in the path of the vehicle, which was as much larger than himself as a good-sized house to a man. He was immediately shot, but the car stopped to load up the carcase and the herd escaped.

Animal parents will sometimes fight against heavy odds to protect their young. Such self-sacrifice by animals, however, seems to be limited to sexual and parental instinct. We cannot imagine animals facing pain for a moral principle, which seems to be an attribute solely limited to man. Perhaps we should also mention the devotion of dogs to their masters, but this again can be attributed to personal affection, rather than to the courage to face danger for a moral issue.

If pain did not exist, most of the supreme acts of heroism which we admire would never take place, and the whole moral side of human life would be grievously impoverished.

Not all pain, however is the result of accidents or violence. Much of it may simply be due to diseases, which the victim has done nothing to incur, and which no human enemy has inflicted. But if we accept the theory that the object of our brief lives is to prepare us for a higher state of service after we die, then we must admit that illnesses may serve a useful end in reminding us of our physical frailty and of the approach of death.

We may indeed observe, both in ourselves and in others, that when we enjoy glowing physical health we are less inclined to think of God and of the object of our lives than when we are struck down by illness and suffer pain. Thus, in this sense also, pain can be a necessary warning of impending danger—the danger of frittering away our lives in the pursuit of pleasure or gain, without giving a thought to its ultimate end.

Human sufferings increase as we grow old, as I know by my own experience. But this also seems to me to be a wise provision, for it reminds us that we have little time left to amend our wasted lives. As a tutor applies more pressure to the student as the final exams draw nearer, so God reminds us of the need for greater moral effort as the end of our lives approaches. We begin, therefore, to glimpse the possibility that pain is an essential ingredient of human existence, both to increase our physical safety, and also to remind us of the brevity of our lives and of the necessity of seriously taking stock of the value of our way of life.

Before leaving the subject of physical pain, we may also for a moment consider its positive value. We have already seen its usefulness in reminding us of the brevity of life, but it also provides us with an immense opportunity for service. The patient endurance of pain, cheerfully, smilingly and indeed joyfully, offers a shining example to all who see it—an inspiring illustration of the victory of the spirit over the body. This indeed may apply to all physical disabilities—lameness, blindness, deafness or any other handicaps. The spirit can rise joyfully supreme over all such suffering and thereby provide a spiritual inspiration which will lead many to righteousness.

We may also record on the credit side of pain, the emotions of compassion, kindness and love which it can evoke in those who observe it. These—some of the most precious of human qualities—owe much to the sight of the joyful and heroic suffering of pain by other people.

✠

Perhaps, however, the most anguished suffering which a human being can endure is bereavement. Could we abolish bereavement in the world which we modelled to our heart's desire? It would seem difficult to do so, because the pain of bereavement is the complement of love. None of us would wish to abolish love, but if we love someone, their death must obviously cause us pain.

To avoid bereavement, everyone would have to die together—an obvious absurdity. Some societies did, indeed, kill the widow when her husband died (though we do not hear of the husband being put to death when the wife died!). This custom seems to have been based on an idea of the continuation of life after death, which was visualized as a further prolongation of an existence similar to the present life. Husband and wife would, therefore, continue to need each other's company.

The avoidance of bereavement is impossible and its acute pain and loneliness is in proportion to our love. The only alleviation which we can conceive is a belief in the brevity of this life, the certainty of its continuance after death, and the omnipresence of a loving God, whose spirit can dwell in our souls. Human love is a foretaste of eternity. It does not end as do youth, pleasure and money. We can still love those who are no longer with us.

But perhaps many people, when moulding a world according to their heart's desire, would ask first of all for more money. Wealth seems desirable for three reasons. Firstly, we think it would enable us to have more pleasures, a better house, a larger car, more electronic gadgets in our homes, or holidays abroad. Yet the thrill of such pleasures lasts only a short time before they lose their novelty. Or perhaps they produce in us a restless discontent, always wanting more parties, more luxuries or bigger cars.

Secondly, some people aspire to become rich out of pride. Their wealth gives them status, is a tribute to their own powers, and enables them to feel condescending towards others. We can hardly ask for more money in our ideal world for this reason. For if it enabled some individuals to feel superior, it would in the process force others to feel inferior. Increasing the satisfaction of some, it would increase the unhappiness and resentment of others. Yet even the prestige achieved by wealth does not last for long. Most of us when young dream of future greatness, but when at length we attain the objects of our ambition, they somehow cease to possess any value. Our tastes have changed, and we no longer find satisfaction in lording it over our fellows who have failed to achieve as much worldly success as we have.

Thirdly, and chiefly among the older half of the population, the desire for money is largely inspired by fear—the dread of poverty in old age when, no longer able to earn, we may have to rely largely on our savings. The fears of old people who can no longer work are understandable. If they have food, clothing and shelter, they may well be content. Their happiness depends more on love than on worldly pleasure—love of one another and of their own young people. While in Britain the state has done much to help the aged, the unhappy corollary is that many families no longer feel obliged to care for their old people. They fail to realize that love is more precious than food or shelter. The state can undertake the latter, but often fails to provide love.

We are perhaps more sophisticated about money than was formerly the case. Monetary inflation and commercial recession have shown us how uncertain and how unreliable money can be. In planning our land of heart's desire, it is no longer enough to say, 'Let's all have a lot more money'. Personally, however, my own impression is that wealth bears little relationship to happiness, and indeed often causes its owner more anxiety than enjoyment. Sudden changes of fortune may, however, be painful. It is difficult for rich people suddenly to become poor or, for that matter, for the poor suddenly to become rich, throwing into confusion a life to which they had become accustomed. The same conclusion has been dramatically confirmed by case-studies of persons who have won the football pools.

I remember a case of an old woman in Texas who owned a plot of land on which prospectors drilled an oil well. Soon the oil royalties began to pour in but, with more wisdom than most of us possess, she refused to change her way of life. The oil company kept paying the money into her bank account, where it remained untouched. She never changed her way of life.

All these considerations apply as much to nations as to individuals. I lived for thirty-six years in the Middle

East, often among the very poorest of the people. Frequently they were desperately short of food and many were dressed in rags. I have seen children picking undigested grains of barley from horse dung in the streets and eating them. No medical facilities whatever existed, a high proportion of babies died and anyone who contracted a serious disease probably failed to recover.

Many families I knew, thirty or forty years ago, lived on about £20 a year, possibly equivalent to £100 at today's rates. Yet the remarkable fact seemed to be that those people were more contented than the populations of the Western nations today. The atmosphere in which they lived had not given them the idea that the accumulation of money was the principal object of human existence.

This is perhaps the end of the whole matter. At least for the first half of our lives, most of us accept without question the mental atmosphere of our society. Only later do we discover that the values which we once accepted without thinking are in fact false. This may perhaps be an exaggerated generalization, for many young people all through history have seen through the vanity of the world, and felt called to give their lives in self-sacrifice and service.

At a recent meeting between employers and employed to discuss an increase in wages, voices from the floor of the hall were reported by the press to have shouted, 'We want to *live*, not just to exist'. This slogan seems to signify the belief that really to live was merely a question of money—a tragic error indeed.

Christ said that he came to give his followers more abundant life, but he was not promising them a rise of wages. He told them not to worry about what they would eat or drink, or what clothes they would wear. The world seeks such things, he added, but, 'Seek ye first the kingdom of God, and his righteousness'.

It is we ourselves who decide whether we are to be peaceful and happy, or anxious, grasping and bitter. This is not a religious exhortation, but a statement of psychological fact. We live in love, joy and peace in proportion to our conformity to the plan of our Creator. He made us to live our lives as a course of training to prepare us for another and a higher existence.

Everything runs most smoothly when it is used in accordance with the instructions of the maker. A petrol engine will not run on crude oil, nor will man, created to live in love, joy and peace by his Maker's design, ever be able to find happiness from the possession of more money. A friend of mine who has much to do with finding employment for school leavers, tells me that young people are no longer so concerned to obtain a large salary, as they were in the 1950s. Most teenagers today are more anxious for 'job-satisfaction' than for money. They want to find fulfilment in the belief that they are doing something really worthwhile. If this be true, it seems to confirm what I said in the introduction. To have a purpose in life, to feel that we are giving valuable service, is the key to contentment.

But we cannot blame God for the martyrdom of man if our unhappiness is due to our own wrong motivation. Christ told us not to worry about money, but to serve God and our fellow men. We ourselves can, therefore, change our unhappiness into contentment if we follow his instructions.

So much for the possibility of abolishing pain and bereavement, and of giving everyone more money. But by far the worst sufferings endured by human beings are inflicted by their fellow men, as the result of wars, violence, cruelty, tyranny or oppression. We cannot blame God for these for he has given us Free Will, leaving us the choice of being cruel to others. God could prevent such wickedness, but only at the cost of destroying our Free Will, and making us into puppets without any personalities of our own.

The cruelty of man to man can only be reduced if human beings become more tolerant, more compassionate and more loving to one another. This cannot be achieved by passing laws or by increasing the punishments of criminals. Revolutions only lead to orgies of violence, after which power is seized by a new set of rulers no less unjust than their predecessors. Moral progress cannot be achieved by compulsion but only by love and co-operation.

We are always complaining. We talk so glibly of the martyrdom of man. We say that if there were a loving God, he could not allow so many sufferings to be inflicted on us. Yet if we suppose that God were to say to us, 'I am going to resign—make the world as you want it', we really cannot think of any improvements!

If we were all kind, loving—and immortal—we might indeed be happy. Nothing less than that would protect us from the vicissitudes of our earthly lives, though any increase in loving kindness and selflessness would alleviate the unhappiness of our society. Perhaps indeed after death we shall find ourselves in a state of universal loving kindness and immortality. But in the meantime, all that we can do to increase our happiness is to raise the moral level of human society—this is indeed a worthwhile purpose for our lives. We cannot blame God for our sufferings. Our martyrdom is due to our own misuse of our Free Will.

6 *The Need for Concealment*

It does not really seem probable that the universe just happened without any cause or Prime Mover. But, as soon as we envisage the existence of a Controlling Power, who wishes to raise us to higher levels so that we can communicate with him, everything seems to fall into place. To my mind at least, reason does not suggest an aimless world, which has come into existence by blind chance. Quite the reverse indeed! It seems to me that reason suggests that the marvellous world we see around us must owe its existence to an all-wise and all-powerful Creator, who knows perfectly well what he is doing.

We can also grasp the basic moral law on which humanity is founded and which controls our whole lives. That law is that good actions carried out under the influence of fear or as the result of coercion lose their moral value. If any word, thought or action is to be considered good, it must have been voluntarily performed with benevolent intentions—that is to say for love. And it must be entirely free from any selfish motive of gain, even the desire to be praised or thanked for it. Thus we also see that good actions must—in order to be qualified as good—be performed in an atmosphere of complete freedom.

This seems to me the first reason why it is necessary for God to conceal himself. If, in some manner or other, he were audibly or visibly to issue his commands, we should all hasten to perform the actions which he ordered, like the ambitious courtiers who surround an absolute monarch. We should inevitably devote ourselves to the task of winning the favour of the divine dictator, on whose goodwill our chances of advancement would depend.

Similarly, of course, if he were visible and openly pronounced his angry intention to inflict agonizing punishment on those who disobeyed his orders, we should avoid antagonizing him in trembling fear of his resentment. But our abstention from crime would not serve to raise the moral level of our lives, because it would be due only to the terror with which his threats inspired us.

There have been many preachers at various times who have attempted to reform the morals of the people by describing the excruciating agonies of hell fire, to be endured for ever and ever by those who did not obey what they claimed to be God's laws. Yet obviously any 'good' actions performed out of fear of eternal torment would not raise the moral level of those who did them. Possibly, here and there, individuals might abandon a frivolous life out of fear of punishment and, having decided to live soberly and to study religion, might later discover the falsity of their first motive, and be led to surrender themselves to God in love.

But if threats of hell-fire may have occasionally frightened a sinner into a more sober life, they did infinite harm to our whole conception of God, by depicting him as an irascible dictator, bent on revenging himself on those of his creatures who did not obey what they were told were his orders. It would become impossible for human beings to feel intimate, loyal and dedicated love for a Ruler, who used savage tortures to punish those who neglected his commands.

The same considerations seem to apply to any attempts to describe heaven and hell, in terms of human life. The descriptions of heaven in the Book of Revelations, with the sound of trumpets, the white garments of the faithful, and the songs of praise, may well be modelled on the rites of the temple in Jerusalem. They may indeed contain secret meanings which we cannot understand. But it does not seem likely that heaven will consist literally of a new City of Jerusalem.

We can scarcely doubt that our future existence will be spiritual, and will result in transforming us into a new creation, which, as long as we remain in this life, we cannot conceive. In any case, even if we could obtain an inkling of this spiritual state in a rare flash of enlightenment, there are no words in human language to depict it. There have, indeed, been saints who perhaps did catch a fleeting glimpse of such spiritual glories, but who subsequently asserted that they were unable to describe them. There were no adequate words in human speech.

It is absurd indeed that such insignificant microbes as ourselves should delight in inflating our own self-importance by challenging God to convince us of his existence. We are confident that he will not do so, and we hope thereby to impress our fellow men without incurring any real danger. We are like naughty school boys who make faces behind the back of their teacher, confident that he will not turn round and see them. They thereby hope to obtain from their comrades the reputation of being challengers of constituted authority, and thus to become objects of admiration to their school-fellows. Their childish minds, utterly unaware of the fact that they are sent to school to acquire knowledge, which will later enable them to lead happy and useful lives, seek only to be flattered and admired by their contemporaries. Their naughtiness and intractability only weary the teachers who are trying to help them, and cause distress and anxiety to the parents who love them. Yet, if they are caught and punished, they are the first to burst into tears and give way to despair.

We are all small boys, grimacing at our Creator behind

his back, and looking round happily to see how the other children are admiring us. We rarely, if ever, pause to consider the object of our existence or the loving care of our Father, who has placed us in school to enable us to grow up and become mature adults, capable of communicating with him. Our minds are too small to grasp such issues. We love 'the praise of men more than the praise of God' (John 12.43). If we pause for a moment to consider this verse, we see how true it is. Our chief ambition is to win popularity—the praise and admiration of men and women—and for this purpose we fritter away our lives uselessly.

However that may be, we can appreciate the law that no good action is of any value, unless it be performed for selfless love. Even a 'good' life in human estimation—a life free from obvious crime and resulting in a respected position among our contemporaries—is of no value, if it is motivated by the wish to win the respect and admiration of other people. The only life possessing any moral value is one lived in complete forgetfulness of ourselves. In order to enable us to live such lives, it is absolutely essential for God to remain invisible. He does not endeavour to prove his own existence to men, he does not court them or argue with them in order to secure their allegiance, as a politician might do when seeking to increase the membership of his party. On the contrary, it is necessary to God's plan for our moral progress, that he conceal his presence.

This is a concept which human beings find difficult to grasp. Our brains are so closely attuned to our own way of life in the material world, that we, perhaps unconsciously, always tend to think of God as an enlarged man. We cannot get away from the very human idea that if he wants us he will either seek to win us over by flattery and promises, or that he will attempt to terrify us into obedience by threats.

The first alternative—the idea that God is courting us to win our favour—only increases our absurd arrogance. For such a situation depicts our Creator as a petitioner, and gives us the initiative to accept his suit, or condescendingly to reject it. We think that we are so clever that we can see through his wiles, and in the process demonstrate how brilliantly intelligent we are.

This ludicrous attitude on our part explains the much emphasized Christian insistence on what is called humility. The quality of humility is not the belief, or even the pretence, that we are inferior in any way to our neighbours. In any case, we have nothing to be proud or ashamed of in our own qualities, if we are clever or stupid, strong or weak. We have nothing which we did not receive from our Maker.

Humility, however, has nothing to do with our fellow human beings. It is simply directed towards God. It is the realization that He is eternal and infinite, a spirit filling, vitalizing and controlling the whole universe, of the limits of which we have no knowledge. We, in comparison, are nothing—tiny animalculae on a speck of matter floating in space. The whole tissue of ideas of ourselves as people whom the Creator wishes to persuade and win over, is seen to be laughably preposterous. Humility towards God turns out to be merely plain realism—a correct appreciation of our actual situation in the universe.

Indirectly, this realistic appreciation will result also in a more modest attitude towards other people. Where all are nonentities, there is no room for any to boast superiority over others. Every form of pride or snobbishness must vanish, whether between individuals, classes or ethnic groups.

In brief, it is essential for God's presence to be concealed, if we are to grow in moral stature by taking our own decisions.

7 *Communication*

Let us assume then that we have reached the conclusion that God exists, that he created the universe, that he originated life, and that he eventually chose one of the living species which he had made and prepared it for further advancement. On this species, man, he conferred a moral sense of right and wrong, the power of self-examination and a feeling of guilt at his inadequate moral performance. He also conferred upon man the power of Free Will, enabling him to choose his own course of action, and thereby to become an individual personality. It was by choosing to perform moral actions, not motivated by gain or fear, that man was to rise to moral levels enabling him to communicate with God.

If, therefore, God was to guide man to higher standards of morality, he must needs do so without himself appearing. We used the comparison of extra-sensory perception to suggest that God could doubtless infuse thoughts into human minds in such a way as to influence their conduct, but without permitting them to know for certain whence the ideas had come.

✠

As has already been mentioned, there are no words in human language adequate to describe divine mysteries. Indeed words confuse as often as they clarify. We cannot complain that God should have made things clearer, because it is precisely our lack of clear understanding which constitutes the training value of our lives. It is we ourselves who have to exercise our freedom of choice, if we are to grow into moral personalities.

✠

The immediate subject which we are discussing is how God communicates with man, especially in view of the fact that he must influence people without their knowing whence the influence comes.

In a previous work[1], I compared God's communications to man with a broadcasting station, which can pass innumerable messages on invisible waves to anyone who has a receiving set and switches it on. The comparison is valid only up to a point. If God were, so to speak, directing a central transmitting station, he could broadcast messages which everyone could receive, perhaps without knowing whence they came. In that case, however, everyone would receive the same message. But the remarkable part about human beings and their intercourse with God is that, if they ask for special help or instructions, they receive an individual reply suited to their personal needs. To most people, such intuitions may only come from time to time. Others, however, seem to live in constant touch with God. The simile of the main transmitting station broadcasting messages to all and sundry does not, therefore, seem adequately to describe human experience.

There are innumerable examples of detailed answers. Individuals, missions, churches or philanthropic institutions tell stories of, for example, financial crises which they have undergone. Contracts or payments for rent have to be met on a fixed date. The whole problem is laid before God. On the very morning on which a payment is due, a cheque arrives in the post from an unknown donor, for exactly the sum required, even down to fractions. The effect is exactly that of a head office to which a tele-

[1] J. B. Glubb, *The Way of Love*

phone call for help has been made, and from which a cheque is received on the correct date.

Much of our incredulity about these events can be traced to our unconscious visualization of God as a large-size man. We feel that he could not possibly handle all the prayers of the world at the same time and give individual replies. If we hear that some institution owed money and that, as a result of prayer, it received the exact amount on the correct date, we say either that it must have been a coincidence, or else that it is impossible.

Our incredulity is doubtless due to the fact that our minds are filled all day long with the affairs of men. If we familiarize ourselves with the chain of logic which I have attempted to trace, we begin to appreciate the narrowness of our own ideas. God created the universe, then originated life. Subsequently he chose one species of living things and conferred upon it a moral sense. All these steps are logical and provide the only reasonable explanation of the world about us. If we truly grasp these marvels, there is no reason to disbelieve the fact that God can communicate with his creatures. Indeed, when we come to think of it from first principles, if he created us and feels for us interest and sympathy, it would seem to be obvious that he would want to communicate with us.

Let us then return to the question as to how this communication can take place. Perhaps the most common reply made by Christians would be 'through the Holy Spirit', a phrase which we shall discuss in a later chapter. In many ways, however, answers to prayer may be thought to resemble extra-sensory perception. We tell God of some trouble in which we find ourselves and ask for his guidance. A short time later the correct course suddenly occurs to us. It is easy to say that the idea was the product of our own brains, but these doubts are inevitable when we remember, as we have already seen, that God's messages must necessarily be untraceable in order to preserve our Free Will. When such things happen frequently, both nowadays and all down the centuries, the possibility that the messages are from God has to be seriously envisaged.

Naturally, persons who wish to receive such messages must take periodical quiet times to think. If we close our minds to such communications and allow ourselves to be constantly preoccupied with anxious worldly thoughts, we cannot register the quiet messages from God. Looking back over the past, we often realize that the message we received, which seemed somewhat dubious at the time, did in fact, when followed, ultimately prove to be the correct solution.

As already explained, if this life is a period of character training, we must ourselves make our decisions, if they are to possess moral value. If God were openly to give us orders, we should lose our Free Will and become the yes-men of a dictator. But, by slipping the correct ideas into our minds, he can guide us through life almost unperceived. Personally I am fully convinced that he does guide us.

By referring our problems to God and awaiting his guidance, we acquire the habit of thinking of him more frequently. We seem to acquire a feeling of his constant presence, which assists us in our daily lives. We cannot boast, swear, threaten or pilfer with Christ looking on. We unconsciously acquire the habit of acting as though we saw him who is invisible.

✠

I have used the similes of radio and extra-sensory perception to convey some ideas to modern readers of how God may perhaps communicate with men. No such ideas of course existed in biblical times, and it is perhaps safer to adhere to the phraseology of the New Testament, which everywhere uses the word 'indwelling'.

The letters of Paul are full of references to the indwelling spirit:

> They that are after the flesh do mind the things of the flesh, but they that are after the Spirit, the things of the Spirit. (Rom. 8.5)

> Ye are ... in the Spirit, if so be that the Spirit of God dwell in you. Now if any man have not the Spirit of Christ, he is none of his. (Rom. 8.9)

> If the Spirit of him that raised up Jesus from the dead dwell in you ... (Rom. 8.11)

> God hath sent forth the Spirit of his Son into your hearts ... (Gal. 4.6)

And so it goes on.

Paul's ideas are simple. He does not worry about precise definitions of dogma to please tidy little human minds, but speaks equally of the Spirit of the Father, the Spirit of Christ or the Spirit. Yet to Paul, the indwelling Spirit was intensely real and vital. He bubbles over with it in his passionate tributes to its power. He and his fellow Christians had experienced it personally and lived by it. He knew that there is something divine in us—or that we are capable of receiving something divine into ourselves. He had himself experienced that this divine something which can live in us, can control our whole lives and reshape our characters.

The early Christian church was deeply inspired by this indwelling Spirit which they had experienced at first hand. They were not concerned to attempt the impossible task of understanding its workings with their human brains, or of defining it precisely in the cramping and restrictive terms of human language.

We shall return to the question of 'indwelling', when we have given more thought to the life of Christ himself.

✠

Having thus early in this book advanced the belief that Christianity consists of the indwelling of men and women by God, it may be of interest, by way of contrast, to examine for a few minutes the rather Victorian quality of respectability. To many people, going to church on Sundays was one of the touchstones of respectability. It was, and perhaps still is, generally considered to be the essential quality of a Christian, thus confusing respectability with Christianity. Perhaps we may say that respectability was indeed a carefully limited form of Christianity, which has occupied a large place in our ways of thought in Britain for the last one hundred and fifty years.

Respectability imposed many restrictions on our outward conduct, such as abstention from murder, theft, adultery, financial dishonesty, lying, drunkenness and swearing. These moral restrictions were of immense value to society. The tradition of always telling the truth gave rise all over the world, to the belief that 'an Englishman's word was his bond'. I remember a former mayor of Nablus in Palestine telling me that before 1914 the Palestinians, when they wished to convince someone of a given statement, would say, 'Word of an Englishman what I say is true'.

Respectability produced the English gentleman of the Victorian age, one of the finest types of character in history. The abandonment of these moral standards, as being bourgeois or middle-class, has reduced our country in fifty years to a low position among the nations. Yet, if we believe that Christianity means the indwelling of God in our souls, we begin to realize that respectability had little to do with Christianity. Even pagan peoples at the height of their national culture could produce honest, straight-forward and honourable gentlemen.

The respectable did not show that humility which is forced upon us when we realize our human nothingness before God. They did not think it wrong to press their own claims to pre-eminence. They were often kind, unswervingly loyal and devoted to duty, but they did not always show compassion to those who were beyond the bounds of their familiar world. They practised few, if any, of the outward vices which disgrace society, yet they largely failed to attain the calm, gentle, selfless and fearless character of the interior Christian. For respectability concentrated on the exterior signs of good conduct, whereas Christianity is an interior condition—God dwelling in our souls.

Now that respectability has largely disappeared from our society, we see the result in the ever-increasing signs of the disintegration of our civilization—the rising crime rate, the loss of respect for marriage, and bribery and dishonesty in business and in public life. We begin to realize the value of respectability to our society. Yet we can see also why it ultimately failed. A code of honour, however rigid, is of inestimable value to a nation, but it is limited to exterior conduct. The respectable failed because they did not go deep enough. Only our self-surrender to God dwelling in our souls can save our civilization.

8 *Son of Man*

We have speculated in the previous chapter as to how God could guide human beings to higher moral levels without issuing direct orders. We concluded that it would be easy for him to do so by inserting ideas in their minds without their knowing for certain whence those ideas came. But in the process of raising mankind to higher spiritual levels, God was not limited to the insertion of ideas in their minds. Another means open to him was to send a perfect man to live upon earth, as an example to the whole human race.

Books are of limited value, for the written word can well be misunderstood. Moreover the mental atmosphere can change, and a book which appeals passionately to one generation will be neglected a hundred years later. In addition, written documents introduce a language difficulty and the possibility of errors of translation.

The influence of a perfect life is, therefore, more powerful and more lasting than the limited inspirations of various prophets or writers. It is indeed obvious in the world about us that example is the most powerful influence in human life. When, therefore, we come to think of it, it seems extraordinary that anyone should be surprised at the fact that God should make use of the example of a perfect Man in guiding us to spiritually higher levels. God is Spirit diffused throughout the whole universe, immortal, infinite, glorious, omnipotent. How was such a Being to speak to such ephemeral, half-animal creatures as ourselves?

The appearance of such a perfect Man was thus undoubtedly the most important event in human history until now. If Christ were to set an example for the whole human race, he must obviously be a man, apparently identical with ourselves. If a god had appeared on earth and had performed marvellous actions, we should not have been inspired to imitate him. We should have shrugged our shoulders and said, 'It was all very well for him, for he was a god. But we mortals cannot of course live a life like his.'

But Jesus was at pains to contradict any such idea. Indeed he told us that we should do even greater things than he had done. John (14.12) says, 'He that believeth on me, the works that I do, he shall do also; and greater works than these shall he do.' This is a most extraordinary statement, and one which seems to receive insufficient attention. Far from claiming divine status, he seems here to tell us that, if we learn from him as his apprentices, we shall do even greater works than he did!

In John 12, he had claimed that he had come as a light into the world, that is as an example which would shed a light which we could all follow. Yet in John 14.10 he said, 'I am in the Father and the Father in me. The words that I speak unto you, I speak not of myself, but the Father that dwelleth in me, He doeth the works. Believe me that I am in the Father and the Father in me.' And in verse twenty of the same chapter, 'Ye shall know that I am in my Father, and ye in me, and I in you.'

It is, of course, absurd for an insignificant little creature like me to discuss the divine mysteries, which have been the study of many of the best intellects for two thousand years. I certainly make no claim to understand, and even less to teach or to lay down the law. But I am an ordinary man of average intelligence in a workaday world. If I venture to express my thoughts, I do so in case they may be of any interest to ordinary people like myself.

When, therefore, I consider the above verses—and many others in the same vein—it seems to me that they can be explained on one basis alone. We are diminutive creatures of flesh, while God is an immortal Spirit. But the Spirit can penetrate us, tiny and carnal as we are, and can inspire us to noble ideals and great deeds. He can, as it were, galvanize us into heroism. If we believe that Jesus was a man, then he would also have been permeable to the Spirit. Is it not reasonable to suggest that our Lord was completely penetrated with, or even possessed by the Spirit?

Many brilliant thinkers for two thousand years have discussed the Incarnation. They are still doing so today. Presumably we all enjoy exercising our natural gifts, whether we be tennis players, beauty queens or intellectuals. There is, however, no justification for arrogance or resentment in these contests. As St Paul says, we have nothing which we have not received, whether we were born with long legs, a straight nose or a subtle brain.

I cannot feel greatly moved by these theological battles, perhaps because my brain is not on their level. But I find it difficult to believe that it is necessary to be an intellectual in order to serve God. For our Heavenly Father loves all his creatures. Would he have created thousands of millions of human beings who yearn to know him, but who are debarred from doing so owing to the inadequacy of their intellects? A universal religion must be attainable by all mankind. The touchstone which, our Lord tells us, separates the sheep from the goats, is not their academic accomplishments, but their love and service to their fellow men. Thus, in his divine wisdom, he has decreed that love is the quality in which we shall be examined. For every human being is capable of love, and no one is debarred by accidents of birth or education from practising love.

William Neil writes, in his *Life and Teaching of Jesus*:

'Perhaps the best corrective to hasty judgement is to

measure these two thousand years against the untold millions of years of man's development. Organized Christianity is still in its infancy, as is the mind of man as he seeks to grapple with truths that could only come to him by revelation. The half has not yet been told and the full implication for human thought and action of the coming of God in Christ has as yet been only dimly grasped by us.'

It seems to me to be part of our modern arrogance that we aspire to explain everything by the light of our tiny intelligences. Personally, therefore, I see no difficulty in accepting that Jesus was God and Man—man by his human nature, but so possessed and penetrated by the Divine Spirit as to reveal to the world a perfect personality. I may be completely wrong, but this theory assists me to try and live with selfless service as the object of my life, without worrying myself over what are called 'intellectual doubts'.

If we could read the gospels afresh with open minds we should, I think, be struck by the way in which they reveal the character of a single and unique, powerful and creative mind. The constant niggling criticisms directed to finding inaccuracies in dates or details, have tended to obscure in our minds the splendid picture of a unique character. Yet all Christ's words and actions have the stamp of the same utterly original and overpowering personality, which shines through the inadequacies of human speech.

The outstanding characteristics of the life of Christ were in complete contrast to those of the Messiah whom the Jews expected. Their lives, like ours, were largely dominated by nationalism, politics and money, and they hoped for a liberator who would lead a rebellion, and establish a powerful and prosperous earthly kingdom by inflicting military defeat on their enemies. In other words, their religious hopes were directed solely to the attainment of better worldly conditions at the expense of other peoples.

Some New Testament commentators have suggested that Christ did share the common Jewish hope of his time that a Jewish earthly kingdom would shortly be set up. Whether he expected the kingdom of God to be set up sooner or later, we do not know. He himself, when asked, replied that the times and the seasons rested with God the Father alone. But that he hoped for a Jewish earthly kingdom seems to me to be completely erroneous. He would never countenance or encourage violence. On the contrary, he said, 'The kingdom of God is within you'—an entirely spiritual conception.

He lived in a world of thought entirely different from that of the Jewish nationalists. Realizing that God was Spirit and that the Spirit could penetrate, even saturate, the human soul, the object of his teaching was to convince mankind that they could thus be indwelt by God. By this means, they would be filled with a new and enhanced vitality, due to their harmonious and conscious co-operation with their Creator, the source of all power.

Luke (2.41–52) gives us the incident of the young Jesus, then twelve years old, listening to and questioning the doctors of the law in the temple, obviously an example of extreme intellectual precocity. When his parents protested, he replied, 'Wist ye not that I must be about my Father's business?' This answer shows that, even at this early age, he had formed ideas of the fatherhood of God. Thereafter we have scarcely any information for about twenty years, except that he 'increased in wisdom and stature and in favour with God and man'. Otherwise, as far as we know, he worked as a village carpenter in Nazareth.

These circumstances, which we usually pass over without much thought, seem to me to convey certain lessons. Firstly they remind us that God is never in a hurry. If we had been the guardians of a boy who, we thought, was to achieve world-wide influence, how anxiously we should have tried to obtain for him the best education, arranging for him to make influential friends and to keep in touch with world events. The years in Nazareth seem to me to show us how trivial are our preoccupations. God, unlike us, is never in a fuss or a hurry. The fact that he grew up in such poor circumstances teaches us the unimportance of our human ideas of rank, wealth and importance. I have no doubt that his social insignificance was deliberately intended to convince us of the vanity of human ideas.

But most significant of all, I believe, is the statement that he increased in wisdom and stature and in favour with God and man. It might at first sight be argued that, if Christ 'had been God', he would automatically have known everything. How then could he increase in wisdom as he grew up? The fact that he did learn as he became older proves that he was a man.

I think that we can also deduce the essential fact that the indwelling Spirit does not increase our knowledge of material facts. Saints are not necessarily chemists, physicists or mathematicians. The Spirit transforms our personalities, making us selfless, affectionate, patient and fearless. Even Christ had to learn his trade as a carpenter.

We have no means of knowing how his thinking developed during this period. We may, however, conclude from what was to follow that he spent much time in thinking about the Fatherhood of God, the state of the world and the object of his own life. When he heard that his cousin, John the Baptist, was baptizing in the Jordan, he went to observe his ministry, and perhaps to seek the answer to his own questionings and meditations. When, after his baptism by John, he emerged from the water, he received a sudden inrush of the Spirit into his soul. So powerful was this visitation that he could only retire into the desert, to think out the implications of this tremendous religious experience, which seems to have convinced him that it was his role to be the Saviour of the world.

The problem was to discover how this part was to be played. The 'temptations' depict three worldly short-cuts to the reformation of mankind. The first of these alternative courses was, by miraculous means, to turn stones into bread. This represents the form of politics with which we are all familiar—to secure popular support by raising everybody's standard of living. Our Lord's reply is as relevant today as it was then: 'Man shall not live by bread alone but by every word which proceedeth out of the mouth of God.' A higher material standard of living does *not* satisfy the longings of the human soul. Only spiritual and moral blessings can make men happy, a fact which most modern politicians seem unable to grasp. The second temptation was to win the allegiance of the people by a publicity stunt. Jumping from a pinnacle of the temple would certainly draw the crowds.

The third temptation was to conquer the world by force, after which he would be able as dictator to compel men to serve God. Violence is always the temptation of the enthusiastic reformer, today as much as ever. But this plan would involve co-operation with the devil in the first stages, in order in the end to establish the kingdom of God. How often have earthly rulers attempted to spread God's word by conquest. But our Lord was fully aware that moral progress cannot be achieved by compulsion but only by voluntary means, that is by kindness, persuasion, example, benevolence and love. It is never justifiable to do evil that good may come.

The result of this solitary period in the wilderness was, therefore, to clear his mind. Neither politics nor force, he realized, could be used to establish the kingdom of God among men. Selfless dedication to service was to be his mission in life. It is intensely interesting to notice that, at the very end of his ministry, the day before his death, he emphasized these conclusions to his disciples. In Luke 22.25–8, we read:

> And he said unto them, 'The kings of the Gentiles exercise lordship over them; and they that exercise authority upon them are called benefactors. But ye shall not be so: but he that is greatest among you, let him be as the younger; and he that is chief, as he that doth serve . . . I am among you as he that serveth.'

Returning from the great religious experience of the temptation in the wilderness, his mind had become quite clear. He had realized that the human race could only be saved by selfless service. Moving to Capernaum on the Sea of Galilee, he commenced his ministry.

9 *The Ministry*

The activities of Christ during his ministry may be considered by us under two headings—teaching and healing.

The basis of his teaching was not complicated. He told everyone in simple language that if they become like little children, they could receive the kingdom of God in their own souls. We may flatter ourselves that we are adults and pride ourselves on our sophistication. We reject with contempt the idea of being like little children. I think the significance of the simile of being like little children is to emphasize the necessity of complete surrender to God. Our personal vanity makes us want to have our own say. When we hear what God requires of us, we like to say, 'Yes, that's all very well, but . . .'. We want to argue, to pit our small created brains against the wisdom of the Creator.

The simile of little children is the easiest illustration of unquestioning acceptance of what we are told. The instructions themselves are simple and must be accepted without any mental reservations. The teaching is that if we decide to serve God without reservation, the kingdom of God will enter our own souls. God is a loving Father, not an angry tyrant. Out of love for the human race and without mankind having done anything to deserve it, he had inaugurated a new era—an era in which God would dwell in the souls of men.

For most people, this suggests 'conversion', a word which merely means a complete turning round through a hundred and eighty degrees to face in the opposite direction. Most of us are more or less completely absorbed in the affairs of this material world. We must do an about-turn, and place the pursuit of money and power behind our backs. If we surrender our lives to God, as a small child accepts whatever its mother says, he will provide for all our needs. This will happen because God will come and live in us. The power and wisdom which created and directs the universe will be available to us in the form of increased vitality, increased joy, increased courage, and increased patience in suffering. Christ's own life shows us what a life is like that has been reborn into this new and divine dispensation.

When we realize that he is offering us a life like his own and telling us in the simplest language how we can achieve it, we appreciate what a mess we have made of our lives hitherto. Our past sins and failures show us how incapable we are alone, and throw us back on God. If we look at them the right way, they can at least cure us of our self-satisfaction.

An interesting feature of Christ's teaching, from which we can learn a lesson, is that he always adjusted his words to his listeners. He was always thinking of them, not trying to show off his own cleverness, or to impress the intellectuals of the time with his own academic status. In other words, he was always thinking of his hearers, not of himself. If his lessons are simple and easily comprehensible, it was because his audience consisted of simple people. It was doubtless also to show us that intellectual accomplishments were not necessary in order to serve God. 'Books', said St Augustine, 'could not teach me Charity.'

The whole teaching of Christ is centred upon God, the key element in every situation. He does not wander off into worldly situations, politics, nationalism, education or war. Give yourselves completely and irrevocably to God, he says, and he will come and dwell in you and direct your lives. God provides for the wild flowers and the birds, far more will he care for you. He will not save you from the sorrows and suffering of human life, but he will enable you to bear them victoriously. Once we are self-surrendered to God, all else automatically falls into place.

His parables provide inexhaustible lessons. On the surface, they offer simple moral teaching, which the most ignorant of his hearers could understand. But even the saints cannot exhaust their profound instruction. All spiritual writing is like that. Every time we re-read it, we discover in it new and deeper meaning.

Many aspects of Christ's teaching will be referred to in later chapters, but one of his sayings may be included here, because it summarizes in one sentence the tragedy of Western civilization. It is contained in Luke 12.15. 'And he said unto them, "Take heed and beware of covetousness: for a man's life consisteth not in the abundance of the things which he possesseth".'

Our present civilization represents the exact reverse of this precept. Success in life is commonly regarded among us as the acquisition of more possessions. To achieve this, promising young people are expected to devote all their energies to a completely self-centred struggle to earn more money and acquire more possessions. Newly married couples wish to acquire a house, a car, a television and every form of material comfort and pleasure. To achieve these material aims, both probably go out to work, and abstain from having children or if they have them, inevitably neglect them, because both father and mother are working in order to acquire more possessions. Many men wear themselves out in the effort to grow rich until, at the end of their lives, they are confronted by the prospect of death and realize that all their millions are utterly valueless.

Our obsessions with money and possessions are not, however, limited to individuals. Commercial companies, trade unions and other corporate bodies are directed almost entirely to the acquisition of more money. Industrial disputes originate from the determination of all parties to obtain more money.

This does not, of course, mean that business is necessarily materialistic. Commerce and industry supply the goods and services necessary to a civilized community. All such activities can be sanctioned if they are carried out as selfless services.

Nor is this materialistic outlook limited to any one nation or political party. Capitalists and communists are both equally obsessed by the desire for money and possessions. Karl Marx saw the amelioration of society in terms of a better distribution of wealth—but he also thought possessions to be the most important factor in human life. Thus we see that communism and capitalism both suffer from the identical error— they see material possessions as the most important object to be pursued in this world. The whole of our modern ways of thought are based on a fundamental mistake—our lives cannot be happy if they are based on the desire for more money and more possessions.

This does not, of course, imply that money is wicked in itself. It is only a means of exchange by which we obtain the necessities of life. It is the duty of every human being to work and to support himself or herself and his or her dependents. But the mental attitude which is poisoning our lives and our whole civilization is the belief that a man's object in life is to acquire more possessions. If we could rid ourselves of this illusion there would be no more industrial disputes, perhaps no more wars.

Happiness cannot be bought with money, but comes unsought if we devote our lives to selfless service, to mutual comradeship and to family affection. Our Lord defined, in a single sentence, the canker at the heart of our civilization, covetousness: 'A man's life consisteth not in the abundance of the things which he possesseth.'

Christ's second form of activity as depicted in the gospels was the helping and the healing of the sick and the demented. At the end of the nineteenth century and the beginning of the twentieth, the recorded miracles of Christ were sometimes represented as disproving the truth of the gospels. Miracles just did not happen, it was argued, and thus the fact that the gospels claimed to record miracles was held to prove that they were just fairy tales.

In recent years, however, we have become much more cautious. The immense increase in healing in answer to prayer, and the extraordinary powers displayed by some people in truly miraculous cures have made it impossible to deny that such apparent miracles *do* occur. We can no longer push aside our Lord's promise that men would do even greater works than he did. We are beginning to realize that we know virtually nothing at all about the effect of spiritual power on the material world.

The miracles recorded in the gospels seem to be only samples or typical cases. In between the specific incidents described, we come across such sentences as, 'Jesus ... went about preaching the good news of the kingdom, and healing all manner of disease and all manner of sickness'.

A generous, tireless giving of health, power, sanity and new life runs through the gospels, showing us the unwearied loving kindness, the deep compassion for all suffering and failure, which characterized the whole life of Christ. These are the qualities which must distinguish our lives if we are indeed to be his followers. For us to attempt to serve in this manner, we have first to implore him to pour into our souls something of his own love and his own sympathy. We do not ask this for our own selfish benefit or consolation, but in order that we in turn may pass it on to others. We can only give what we have received from him. Our own personal resources are valueless. But a ceaseless death to ourselves is essential if we are to act as conveyors of God's compassion to the world.

We may perhaps ask ourselves whether those whom we meet in our daily lives go on their way more or less comforted or in peace as a result of speaking to us. Do they leave us stronger in their faith in God or weaker? Are we spreading the peace of God and the love of Christ to those with whom we come in contact, or do we leave them more worried and depressed than before? As Evelyn Underhill writes in her little book, *Light of Christ*:

> He touched the unclean, dined with the wrong people: He accepted the love and fellowship of a sinner (that most wonderful of all remedies for the wounds of sin). He loved with God's love and so went straight to the point: What can I do to restore my fellow-creatures and how?

10 *The Credibility of the Gospels*

Doubtless the principal effect of the ministry of Jesus was the result of his own personality. 'And all bare him witness, and wondered at the gracious words that proceeded out of His mouth' (Luke 4.22). Further on in the same chapter we read, 'and they were astonished at His doctrine for His word was with power'. 'And the people sought Him and came unto Him, and stayed Him, that He should not depart from them.' And in Matthew 7.29: 'For He taught them as one having authority, and not as the scribes.'

He was followed everywhere by huge crowds, so that he often had no chance to sit down or to eat. In Mark 2.4, we read of the palsied man whose friends could not reach Jesus because of the crowd. So they climbed on the roof, stripped off the roofing material and lowered the sick man into the house. In John 7.45, the temple police officers are sent by the chief priests to arrest our Lord while he is speaking in the temple, but returned without him. The chief priests asked why they had not brought him, and the police officers answered, 'Never man spake like this man'.

In John 8 we are told the story of the woman taken in adultery, who was brought to him by the scribes and Pharisees, in the hope that they would be able to trap him into saying something contrary to the law of Moses. 'And Christ lifted himself up and said unto them, "He that is without sin among you let him cast the first stone".' Then these professional lawyers and church dignitaries, without another word, slipped away one by one. There must surely have been something commanding and noble in his personality which thus overawed all the expert hecklers.

Matthew (22.46) tells us, 'No man was able to answer Him a word, neither durst any man from that day forth ask Him any more questions.' These men who did not dare to ask him any questions were graduates of the highest schools of theology and philosophy, while he was a village carpenter. Must there not have been something majestic in such a personality, to whom the professional intellectuals were afraid to speak?

The common people worshipped him as a hero. The women cured of a haemorrhage said, 'If I can but touch his clothes I shall be healed'. In Matthew 8.5–8 we read of the Roman centurion who came to him about his sick servant. Our Lord replied, 'I will come and heal him,' but the centurion answered, 'Lord, I am not worthy that thou shouldst come under my roof.' Should we expect an officer of the imperial army garrisoning a country to say that he was not worthy that a village carpenter should enter his house? Must there not have been some overwhelming dignity about this carpenter?

Even those who hated him paid tribute to his courage, his frankness and his honesty. Matthew (22.15–16) tells how the Pharisees sent their disciples to him to trap him. They began by saying, 'Master, we know that thou art true, and teachest the way of God in truth, neither carest thou for any man: for thou regardest not the person of men.'

It was for this courage, openness and frankness that the common people heard him gladly and flocked to him from every quarter. William Neil, in his *Life and Teaching of Jesus*, says: 'The outstanding character of Jesus is his authority. In Jesus' preaching there was an entirely new note of personal certainty and assurance.' No matter how closely his followers were drawn to him by their love and devotion, they always felt that they were separated from him by an impassable gulf. 'They had the sense of being in the presence of someone from another world,' says William Neil.

The reader will have noticed that I have hitherto accepted the gospels as accurate. Perhaps at this stage I should include some explanation of the reason.

It is generally estimated that St Mark's Gospel was produced some thirty-five years after the crucifixion. The delay can probably be explained if we appreciate that the majority of the disciples were uneducated men. Moreover, we must realize that writing books was in those days a formidable task, very different from the easy process of today, with our ample supplies of paper, pens and typewriters, and our many publishers. In ancient times, it meant writing laboriously by hand on long scrolls of parchment, and all that labour produced only one copy.

The first Christians were mostly poor and ignorant, but they were fired by an immense and passionate devotion to a Person, whom they had known intimately and about whom there was something which had convinced them that he had come from another world. His death had plunged them into the deepest despair. His resurrection had filled them with irresistible joy and fearless courage. It must be remembered that the coming of the Holy Spirit, as depicted in Acts 2, was only ten days after the Ascension or seven weeks after the Resurrection.

The result of the gift of the Holy Spirit was the sudden and amazing transformation of the disciples from a terrified little group into an utterly fearless body of men, who did not hesitate openly to defy the Sanhedrin, the body which had contrived the crucifixion of their Master.

If we suggest that the coming of the Holy Spirit was a myth, we cannot account for the extraordinary transformation of the believers nor for their fearless defiance, firstly of the Jews and then of the Roman Empire. Moreover, their sudden transformation disproves, in retrospect, any theories that the disciples might have invented the Resurrection, or stolen and concealed the body of Christ. It is not credible that men and women should have heroically faced martyrdom for what they knew to be a shady trick which they had worked.

The immediate question which we were discussing, however, is why the gospels were not written and published for another thirty or thirty-five years. The delay can doubtless be partly explained by the difficulty to poor people of writing and publishing books in Palestine in the first century. In this connection, however, there are two points to which I should like to draw attention.

I lived for thirty-six years in the Middle East and I subsequently spent eighteen years in studying and writing books on the history of the area. The experience which I thus gained has impressed two factors on my mind. The first of these is that uneducated people in the Middle East have retentive memories, which to us seem miraculous. In tribal disputes, I have heard illiterate men give descriptions of incidents which had occurred thirty or forty years before, and of which the smallest details were still perfectly remembered by them. 'I saw Hamad riding down the hill with a hawk on his wrist. He was riding his old grey mare, which was remarkable for the fact that she had a patch of black hair on one of her ears.' This evidence referred to an incident forty years before.

It may be that these extraordinary powers of memory can be attributed to the fact that these people's minds were not overburdened by masses of extraneous facts forced into their minds at school, and were thus solely occupied with their own lives. Perhaps also our memories have been weakened by the fact that we write everything down.

I mention the fact of the amazing memories of simple

people in the Middle East to emphasize that a delay of thirty-five years in the publication of the first complete written gospel does not mean that the incidents related might have been forgotten. Indeed the situation might be described the other way round. The necessity of producing complete written accounts of the life of Christ did not appear urgent because so many people were still alive who remembered every detail. We do not indeed know when the first written accounts were recorded. There were certainly numerous written sources available, possibly notes by many different witnesses, before the first complete gospel was produced.

The second point to which I would draw attention is a question of different historical styles between the Middle East and the modern West. A Western biographer today is above all anxious to obtain accurate 'facts', such as the dates of birth, marriage, promotion or death of his subject; his education, professional status, the opinions of friends and contemporaries, the good fortune or the unlucky chances suffered by his subject in his career. A biographer who gave a wrong date would be automatically rejected by all.

Middle Eastern writers adopt a different style. They are not very interested in dates and may well forget to mention the date of birth. Their biographies consist largely of anecdotes and of reported conversations. These, it is considered, depict with far greater accuracy the character and the accomplishments of their subject, than mere accuracy in giving dates, facts, physical appearance and the colour of eyes or hair, which are often completely omitted.

Some modern European writers like to state that we have no real biography of Jesus Christ. We do not even know his date of birth or his physical appearance, which none of the gospels attempt to describe. The anecdotes of which the gospels consist can probably, in the absence of the basic facts, be treated as myths. These critics are doubtless unaware that this is the style in which all Middle Eastern history has been written.

Seven or eight hundred years after Christ, the Arabs had established an immensely wealthy and highly sophisticated empire, extending from the south of France to India and China. This empire produced a large number of writers and historians, universities, colleges, libraries and centres of learning. Voluminous histories and biographies were written, telling the story of the empire and of the Muslim states and their rulers. All are written in a style resembling more closely the narratives of the gospels than the work of modern biographers. In other words, they contain innumerable anecdotes and adventures vividly illustrating the personalities of their heroes and the distinctive features of their cultures, but rarely including physical descriptions of the people involved. Such was not the literary fashion of those times.

11 *The Turning Point*

It gradually became evident that, although immense crowds were emotionally carried away by the power and the love of Jesus, few were ready really to abandon themselves *completely* to the service of God. The rich young ruler sincerely regretted that he could not join the followers of our Lord because he was very wealthy and had to take care of his property.

The parable of the sower emphasizes the fact that Christ realized that most human beings were too engrossed in their worldly occupations. Some heard the good news, but failed to understand it and gave up. Some received it with joy, but were cowed and frightened when they were exposed to ridicule or persecution. Some were unfruitful because of the attraction of money-making and worldly business. Only a few bore fruit, some an hundredfold, some sixty, some thirty. Our Lord was never satisfied with those who put their hands to the plough and looked back. He required total dedication, which, it gradually became apparent, most men had not the courage to give.

Our interest at this stage is roused by the question whether this result was unforeseen by him. It does seem possible that he was gaining experience as he went along. Had he hoped to carry the people with him, and was he disappointed by their lethargy, their cowardice and their worldliness? Some may brand such a suggestion as blasphemy and say, 'If Jesus was God, of course he must have known everything'. Yet in Hebrews 5–8, we are told that he learned 'obedience by the things which He suffered'.

We have already seen that the significance of Christ's

life to us, if we regard it as an example of how to live, lies chiefly in the fact that he was a man. Paul, in Hebrews 4.15, definitely says: 'We have not a high priest which cannot be touched with the feeling of our infirmities, but was in all points tempted like as we are, yet without sin.' May we speculate that the Spirit which dwelt in him did not reveal to him intellectual knowledge about the world, but led him on and guided him, revealing to him day by day what he was to do next? Indeed Christ himself had told his followers not to worry about the future, but to live one day at a time. The indwelling Spirit which filled his whole soul made it impossible for him to sin, but did not impart to him superior intellectual knowledge which would have alienated him from his fellow men.

He seems to have gradually realized the cowardice, the weakness and the worldliness of the human race. As had occurred after the spiritual experience at his baptism, he decided to make a 'retreat' into quiet country for a period of rest and meditation. The constant rush and clamour in which he lived made calm thought difficult. Even to offer his daily prayer and communion with God he was obliged to rise a great while before dawn and to go out alone into the hills. Consequently, taking with him only a few of his closest disciples, he moved to the lower slopes of Mount Hermon in a non-Jewish area. Here he seems to have re-assessed his ministry, reaching the conclusion that his task could only be completed by his own suffering and death. This new religious experience was marked by the transfiguration, a religious ecstasy produced by his resolve to surrender himself unreservedly to the agony and humiliation which he now realized that his mission demanded. The phenomenon of a dazzling brightness of the face after religious ecstasy is reported of Moses and of many saints in history.

This new re-assessment of his mission is marked

by complete resolution to give himself entirely to God's service, although he was perfectly aware that this would result in his humiliation, torture and death (Mark 10.32–4).

Even as the end of his ministry approached, we find the apostles disputing with one another as to which of them should be the greatest. How deeply distressing it must have been to him to realize that, after his close association with them for two years or more, James and John, his nearest disciples, had no idea of what his preaching meant. They were still arguing with one another about their precedence when he set up what they still imagined would be an earthly kingdom. We have a vivid picture of our Lord walking ahead alone up the road from Jericho to Jerusalem, aware that he was going to his death. Behind him came the disciples, anxious, timid and bewildered.

Those days must have been an intensely emotional experience for the disciples. They were terrified of going to face the authorities in Jerusalem, as dissidents in Germany under the Nazis would have been. The ensuing few weeks must have been for them a profoundly traumatic experience. Even if the first complete gospel was not published until some thirty-five years later, it is impossible that these men could have forgotten the experience they had gone through, and which the gospels so vividly describe.

When confronted with a perplexing situation, in which we are tempted to criticize the action adopted by others, it is often useful to consider what the result would have been if events had taken an opposite course. Christ deliberately went up to Jerusalem, knowing that he would be tortured and put to death.

Once he had decided that he would have to face death,

Jesus never looked back. But could there have been another way out? Perhaps he could have reached a compromise solution with the religious authorities, if he had promised in future to observe the minutiae of the Mosaic Law, and to refrain from making any derogatory remarks about the religious establishment. By this means he could have 'saved' his life and been able to continue his preaching and healing, even if on a restricted scale. Perhaps he could have continued his work in Galilee, if he had promised never to return to Jerusalem.

A moment's thought will convince us that this would not have been possible. The core of his message was that God was Spirit and that this Spirit could actually penetrate and indwell human beings, on condition that they opened themselves unconditionally and unreservedly to him. He was convinced that the Spirit dwelt in himself and that he and his Father were one. Thus we may say that the good news which he brought was incarnation—the fact that the Spirit could dwell in men.

But he did not limit this relationship to himself. He promised that both he and the Father would dwell in his followers, who would be able to do the same works as he had done, and even greater works than his. He was to be the first of many brethren (Romans 8.29). The only condition by which men could receive the Spirit to dwell in them was that they should be 'born again', start a new life entirely, directed by God and not devoted to their own selfish interests. This message was strange to men of the world, but was simplicity itself.

But the Jewish religious authorities claimed that men could obtain their salvation by carefully following the Mosaic Law, which involved a great many complicated regulations, regarding washing, purification, Sabbath observance and numerous other rules. Our Lord's denunciation of the religious leaders was based on the accusation that they could observe all the regulations, and yet indulge in financial sharp practice and grow very rich. If he had compromised and agreed to tell people that they must observe all the ritual, the perfect simplicity of his message —*Give yourselves unreservedly to God, and his Spirit will live in you*—would have been obscured and confused.

Perhaps he could have moved to Syria or Lebanon, or to the Gentiles in Asia Minor or Europe. But if he had 'saved' his life by going to live in another country, would not the Pharisees and Sadducees have been triumphant? Would they not have claimed that, after all his fine talk, when it came to a showdown he had run away?

Most of us will, I think, agree that such a solution was unthinkable. The decision which he took after the retreat on Mount Hermon was inevitable. The delivery of his message could only be completed by his death. The need for total self-donation had been the key to all his teaching. His followers must give everything, including their lives. If he had tried to save his life by running away, his followers would never have felt themselves obliged to give more than he had given.

We cannot expect completely to understand the life of Christ by the use of our human intellects, chiefly because our minds are so saturated with worldly ideas. Our points of view are inevitably limited to our deeply engrained human attitudes. Yet his message was perfectly simple and no intellectual accomplishments are necessary to enable us to comprehend it. In John 7.17, our Lord said that if any man would do God's will, he would know whether the doctrine was of God. And what did he say was God's will? That we should love God with all our hearts and minds, and our neighbours as ourselves.

In other words, we are not to try and find God by using our own brains, but if we obey his command to love him and our fellow men, we shall *know* that his teaching is true. And how shall we know? Because his spirit will enter us and live in us and will direct our lives. 'Don't try and reach God with your understanding. That is impossible. Reach him in love. That is possible,' writes Carlo Carretto in his *Letters from the Desert*.

There does not therefore seem to me to be any other explanation necessary for the crucifixion. Christ had challenged the forces of evil in the lives of worldly men—not necessarily irreligious men, for the Pharisees were pious in their way, but they compromised by observing the outward ceremonies of religion, while living self-centred lives and pursuing money and power. There was no possibility of half-measures in the teaching of Jesus. All must be born again if they were to realize the kingdom of heaven on earth.

The earliest Christians, however, were Jews, who had been brought up on the Old Testament and the Mosaic Law. Traditional Judaism had represented God as being frequently angry, like an earthly ruler. From primitive times they had sought to appease his anger by animal sacrifices, and had built up the belief that God would be gratified by the slaughter of an ox or a sheep. The sins of the offender could be transferred to the animal, the blood of which could thus be said to wash away sins.

It is easily understandable that the first Jewish Christians should see in the death of Christ a sacrificial offering, already foreshadowed in their temple sacrifices. They saw him as the Lamb of God, and those sinners, who through him were pardoned, as being washed in the blood of the Lamb—a formula which has survived to our own times.

Yet, if we attempt to analyse this idea, we find that it seems to contradict the teaching of our Lord himself. For one of the principal features of his teaching was that God was a loving father, not an irascible dictator. The idea that God would be appeased by the gift of an ox or a sheep was completely primitive and at variance with all his teaching.

Moreover he identified himself with the Father who, he claimed, dwelt in him. He himself always complied with God's will. How then could this loving Father obtain satisfaction from the torture and death of his Son, who identified himself with him? All these ideas seem to us primitive and anthropomorphic, picturing God as an angry tyrant whose wrath can only be appeased by bloodshed.

Yet, if we abandon these ancient Jewish symbols, we can still see—in fact we see more clearly—that Jesus was the Saviour of the world. For men in those times often (though not always) visualized God as an angry despot. Christ gave us an entirely new outlook. He told us that God was a loving Father, who wished us to love him and one another, and who would give us the indwelling strength to do this, if we gave ourselves entirely to him. The only thing the Father required of us was complete self-surrender to him—a surrender so total and so final that it resembled a new birth. God could not effect this transformation in people who were half-hearted and spent a large part of their lives in the pursuit of wealth, power, or pleasure.

It will be seen that Christ's message was purely spiritual, and was concerned with the indwelling of the Spirit in man. Any theories of the death of Christ as an appeasement to an angry God, seem totally contrary to his teaching. The word 'spirit' is capable of many uses in the confusion of human speech. The whole conception of spirit and spiritual, the very basis of Christianity, will be discussed in a later chapter.

✠

Perhaps the discovery of electricity has transformed our physical lives more than anything else in the last hundred years. Yet it is surprising to realize that no one knows exactly what electricity is. We know how to produce it and how to use it, without exactly understanding its nature. Entering a dark room, we switch on the light, without worrying about the nature of electricity. In a similar manner, we can see plainly that the life, death and resurrection of Christ have transformed the world. We can ourselves experience this transformation if we are ready to dedicate our lives to his service and that of our neighbour. Like the electric switch, it works, and we can make use of it to fill our lives with light and to devote ourselves to the service of our fellow men.

My speculations on the subject of the exact significance of the sacrifice of Christ are, therefore, I humbly admit, unnecessary and futile. Belief in God and in Christ works —and that is enough.

12 *Utter Self-giving*

After his retreat for meditation in a non-Jewish area, our Lord had been convinced that there was no alternative to his own torture and death. The reward of his renewed complete and utter self-abandonment had been the spiritual ecstasy which we call the transfiguration. He had always spoken with complete frankness and had told the world that love and service to God and man was the purpose of life. The authorities were pre-occupied with politics, power and money, as are our leaders today. A head-on collision was inevitable.

At the last supper, he instituted a little ceremony by which he was to be remembered. Not a splendid ritual, with gorgeous vestments and pealing music, but a common little everyday meal, a piece of bread and a sip of wine. Once again he showed God's satisfaction with the poor and the humble things of life, as he already had shown them by being born in a stable and by working as a village carpenter.

Then ensued a staggering incident to which today we seldom see reference—the washing of the feet of his followers. In John 13.4–5, we read that 'he laid aside his garment and tied a towel round his waist, poured some water into a basin and washed the feet of his disciples. He knew that in a few hours he would be tortured to an agonizing death. Yet he dedicated his last hours with the friends he loved to this humble service. We are perhaps not quite happy with this story. We are so preoccupied with our own status and with our dignity that we find this acted parable awkward. For its meaning is inescapable. It is totally destructive of personal vanity, of our constant preoccupation to win the praise of other people or to increase our own importance.

In his *Readings in St John's Gospel*, William Temple makes rather a subtle point. We do not really want our God to be humble. We should like him to glory in his goodness and his greatness. Then we also might be entitled to pride ourselves on our moral achievements—as the Pharisees did. But to servants of Jesus Christ this is impossible. We worship one who himself rendered menial service to common men. If our worship is genuine, every form of human pride is eliminated.

This incident *must* be accurate. Who could ever invent the story of a great leader and hero spending his last hours in washing people's feet? It illustrates in an overpowering manner how essential he thought it to be that we should realize our own nothingness.

The story also emphasizes by this example the duty of rendering service. 'The Son of Man came not to receive service but to give it' (Mark 10.45). But our humility does not only mean the giving of service. Our minds are so skilful at making excuses for ourselves and deceiving our souls! Even when we do behave with apparent humility, we feel proud of being humble. The only solution is selflessness—entirely to forget ourselves through absorption in our service. In case there could be any doubt of the significance of his action, he explained its intention in the clearest terms: 'I have given you an example that ye should do as I have done . . . I am among you as one that serveth' (John 13.15, Luke 22.27).

Probably few of us spend enough time thinking of the Passion in the garden of Gethsemane. On the one hand, the scene seems to have been recorded to encourage us and to set us an example. It shows once again that Christ was a man, tempted in all things just as we are.

He knew in a way that his torture and death were inevitable. Yet at this very last moment he was tormented by a ray of hope. 'Father, if thou be willing, remove this cup from me: nevertheless not my will but thine be done.' It is anguishing even to read of this temptation—this agony of hope—perhaps after all I will not have to face it. This is *fear*, from which even he was not exempt.

The whole of this episode seems to me to be another example of the basic fact that if he had not been a man, his life would not have helped us. 'He was in all points tempted like as we are.' For any of us who are called to face an ordeal, anticipation is often the worst agony. If he had been a god, pure and simple, he would not have suffered from the anxiety of anticipation. It is infinitely consoling to us, when we face in terror an unexpected ordeal, to know that even our Lord was afraid.

The biblical account is almost too painful to read. So intense was Christ's interior struggle that he poured with sweat. But quickly he recovered himself from his weakness. The Spirit re-asserted itself—Luke says that an angel comforted him. When he rose to his feet, he was calm and resolute once more. For the next few hours he endured with quiet serenity the last dregs of the cup of humiliation and agony. No contrast could be more moving than that between the jealousy and vindictiveness of the Chief Priests, the slippery manoeuvres of the politician Pilate, and the dignified majesty of the Prisoner.

Writers have often seen in the passion an epitome of the ending of many human lives. The passionate prayer of terror, not perhaps for the life of the person praying but possibly from the fear of bereavement, at the bedside of a dying husband, wife or child. 'O God, let not this thing happen! O Lord, I implore thee, spare the life of my love. O God, I cannot face life alone. If possible let this cup pass from me.' But the prayer goes unanswered, and we have to face life again with our anguish. Many victims of such agonies, whether in the endurance of their own physical pain or of the anguish of bereavement, have seen their sufferings as a contribution offered by them to the sufferings of Christ. At least we can feel that it leaves us no cause for complaint when we are called to suffer. What right have we to protest, when the perfect God-filled man endured such tortures, although he had never done anything wrong?

At least the account of Gethsemane disposes of the primitive Old Testament idea that suffering in this life is a direct punishment of our own sins. It is extraordinary how hard this theory dies. How often we still hear the complaint, 'Why did my poor husband have to suffer so much, when he had always been such a good man?'

Some of the saints have achieved the moral level of welcoming and rejoicing in their sufferings, as presenting them with something which they can humbly offer as a tribute to him. We too can only lay our little trials and suffering at his feet. There is no need for me to recount the details of the trial and crucifixion of Christ, which are fully narrated in the gospels. The motive of this book is to seek for a worthy purpose for our own lives, not to psycho-analyse the mental processes of Annas, Caiaphas or Pilate.

✠

I have no doubts about the resurrection. Even the outward superficial evidence is irrefutable. It is absurd to suppose that the disciples stole his body and then joyfully faced hatred, imprisonment and martyrdom in order to cover up their shady deception.

After the crucifixion, a tiny group of men and women were hiding in an upper room in Jerusalem. They expected that the authorities, having killed their leader, would arrest his followers and kill them also and finally extirpate what they regarded as a troublesome sect. They did not for a moment expect their Master to rise from the dead. The glorious exhilaration in which they had lived for nearly three years made their present despair all the blacker. They had not quite understood all he said, but were hoping for an earthly kingdom in which they would be the 'King's Privy Council'. But whatever happened, the magnetism of his personality had supported them, and now he was dead. Nothing but agony and misery was left.

Then, utterly unexpectedly, he suddenly appeared among them. Even so, those who did not personally see his first appearance refused to believe the account given them by their comrades. But then, almost in a flash, when they realized what had happened, they were instantaneously filled with an immense joy. They fearlessly proclaimed his name in the streets and before the very Chief Priests who had crucified their Master. Defying not only the Jewish establishment but the Roman Empire, they set out to conquer the world.

In considering this miraculous transformation, we must remember that these were all ignorant and uneducated working men. The age in which they lived, however, was not an age of barbarian ignorance. It was, on the contrary, a period of high culture and of extreme sophistication. It was an age of great imperial military power but also of wide culture, literature and philosophy. How could a dozen poor working men dream of defying such a mighty and ancient civilization?

Only a few days before, when their Lord was arrested, they had all ignominiously deserted him and run away. Obviously something had happened to transform these trembling cowards into utterly fearless heroes and martyrs. The fact that they knew that their Master was still alive offers the only satisfactory explanation of their transformation. Then, a few weeks later, came the gift of the Holy Spirit at Pentecost and the speaking with strange tongues.

At the beginning of the present century, the belief that

material science would soon discover 'everything' led to considerable scepticism regarding the New Testament miracles, the resurrection and the coming of the Holy Spirit at Pentecost. But in the last fifty years, a considerable reaction has taken place. Examples of miraculous healing have become almost commonplace. Traditions of people being seen after the deaths of their bodies have always existed, though possibly dismissed with contempt by materialists. Yet such reports continue. I have quoted elsewhere[1] the account given by Canon J. B. Phillips, translator of the gospels, of how, a few days after the death of C. S. Lewis, he was visited by the latter. 'While I was watching television,' writes Canon Phillips in his book *Ring of Truth*, 'he "appeared" sitting in a chair within a few feet of me and spoke a few words which were particularly relevant to the difficult circumstances through which I was passing. He was ruddier in complexion than ever, grinning all over his face . . . I had not been thinking about him at all. I was neither alarmed nor surprised. He was just there as large as life.'

Perhaps one of the most striking developments of recent years has been the occurrence of incidents in which the Spirit has fallen upon gatherings of worshippers, often accompanied by speaking in strange tongues. The Charismatic Movement, which is non-denominational, has given rise to a new impetus of revival through the Spirit. The Pentecostals likewise often show wonderful results although they unfortunately are a separate denomination. People who are convinced that only the material world exists can completely close their minds to all such spiritual manifestations—this is part of our divinely given Free Will. Personally, however, I am completely convinced of the truth of the resurrection of Christ and of the pouring out of the Holy Spirit and the speaking of tongues at Pentecost.

[1] J. B. Glubb, *The Way of Love*

When considering the progress of Christianity since the crucifixion of Christ, we must always remember that two thousand years is a negligible period in the history of the world or of mankind. If we believe that God is slowly raising mankind to a moral status which will enable them to communicate with him, we must be prepared to find many crude and primitive ideas in the development of human beliefs about God, some of them throwbacks to pre-Christian customs.

We have already frequently noticed the human tendency to think of God as a superman, though the New Testament is singularly free of such misconceptions. Christ taught that God was Spirit, and that the Spirit could dwell in or permeate human beings. His description of God as our Father was intended to depict him as affectionate and deeply concerned in our affairs. He stated that he was in the Father and the Father in him and that both would be in us, if we devoted ourselves to his service. The full meaning of these statements is not clear to us as long as we remain in this material world. Our insignificance in comparison to the Creator of the Universe has been repeatedly referred to in these pages. To imagine that our tiny brains can understand God is laughable.

When we see crude anthropomorphic ideas expressed in the religious phraseology which we have inherited, we are not thereby justified in saying: 'There you are. The whole thing is obviously rubbish.' Rather must we realize that man is still growing up. When we say in the creed that Christ ascended into heaven and sits on the right hand of God the Father, we are obviously using a metaphor, comparing God to an earthly being, whose son and heir sits on the right of the throne. I do not know if those who drafted this wording were consciously using a simile, or really visualized God as sitting on a throne, but the New Testament continually emphasizes the fact that God is Spirit, and Spirit which fills the whole world would obviously not need to sit on a throne! Such simple metaphors need not disturb us.

Briefly, the result of Our Lord's teaching seems to have been: firstly, that God is a benevolent Father, not an irascible dictator; secondly, that god is Spirit filling the whole world around us, but also prepared to dwell in a special way in those people who give themselves heart and soul to his service. We can perhaps compare God to the atmosphere, which envelops us on the outside, and also fills our lungs on the inside. We thus find ourselves faced once again with that difficult word 'spirit', to which it will be worth our while to dedicate a new chapter.

13 *The Spirit*

Many people are more or less familiar with the story of the life of Christ. To some, he is the ideal model for human life, but he died two thousand years ago. To others, his life is a tragic example of martyrdom. But both these classes of people seem to me to miss the principal result of his teaching, which was based on the fact that God is Spirit, and that the Spirit can live in us and direct and control our lives. Spirit is a word constantly used by religious writers, but the exact meaning of the word is illusive. It is the object of this chapter to consider its meaning more closely.

Spirit, used in a religious sense, is difficult to define in human speech. Nevertheless it is something most real and basic to human life. Our experience of it may be occasional and fleeting, or it may entirely permeate and transform our lives. Obviously it is not material, and cannot be seen or touched. Those whose minds are entirely absorbed by the superficial and passing circumstances of their daily lives may never admit it to their thoughts or may contemptuously dismiss it as irrelevant, that is to say of no value in the acquisition of money or power. But those who open their minds to it by dedicating their lives to the service of God, find it to be a continual source of strength and power which, quickly or slowly, will transform their own personalities.

Belief in the Spirit is therefore the result of experience. Those who wish to give their lives in love and service to God and their neighbours will open their souls to its quiet, silent influence until it becomes their guiding light. But they cannot define it in precise terms comprehensible to human reason. Not only is it something which they feel and know, but it (unknown to them) radiates from them to others with whom they come in contact. No amount of human cleverness can define it, yet it sheds on all around the gentle, humble glory of saintliness.

Nor, it must be realized, does it imply the neglect of our worldly duties or a fatalistic resignation to whatever may happen. On the contrary, the Spirit has behind it the same almighty power which created the universe. The saints have often been the most energetic persons of their time, travelling to far countries or working day and night in the slums or in the prisons of their own nation. For the sole pre-occupation of persons filled by the Spirit is God, and the furtherance of his purposes for mankind. To them the word means an immense devotion and an immense attraction which drives them to service with an irresistible energy which they feel but cannot explain in human terms.

Lest so vague and indefinable a concept as Spirit should seem to us cold and impersonal, our Lord used 'Our Father' as an alternative description of God. The two definitions taken together balance one another—the warm, benevolent personal relationship of a father, with the ubiquitous, all-penetrating *something* which fills our own souls and the world around us—Spirit. 'We are all in Him and He is enclosed in us,' wrote Mother Julian of Norwich.

I am no theologian but in my humble opinion it appears that to set up this system of Spirit dwelling in human beings, and to explain it clearly to men was one of the principal objects, perhaps *the* principal object, of Christ's life on earth. It is doubtless true that the Spirit spoke by the prophets in pre-Christian times, but ordinary people believed that prophets were rare and exceptional mortals. Indeed there had been no prophets for a long time before Christ was born. But it did not seem to occur to them that the Spirit could live in and inspire ordinary men and women.

It was Christ himself who first made this plain for all to see. The Spirit is available as a guide, a strengthener, a support and a purifier for every single human being alive. Every man and woman has a divine seed implanted in his or her soul. As long as our minds are *solely* preoccupied with the ever-changing circumstances of the material world, the seed seems to lie dormant, though its presence makes it impossible for us to be completely at ease in the material world. For man is both animal and spiritual, and his mind cannot rest in peace while only one half of his make-up is developed. As soon, however, as he decides to give himself entirely to the service of God and his neighbour, the Spirit begins to take charge of his life, vivifying the divine seed which lies dormant in his soul. As Evelyn Underhill writes in her book *The Golden Sequence*, 'the very heart of all personal religion is the tendency of the created spirit to union with that Spirit–God'.

This Spirit should not be thought of as an influence sent to us from another world but as an intimate, calm yet powerful presence in our inmost selves. The fact that our minds are so often restricted to thinking of human and material factors makes it difficult for us to think of a universal Spirit, dwelling so closely within us as to be part of our very selves. Yet this is only a human limitation. For God *is* Spirit and the Spirit is God himself, who controls, inspires and directs everything that happens to us throughout our lives.

The Spirit, says Evelyn Underhill again, is 'the Object, not of philosophic speculation, but of direct and awe-struck experience'. It is not some vague theory of the general immanence of God in nature, but a powerful invasion from another order of existence, which nevertheless finds hidden within ourselves a secret congenial element springing to life at the divine touch, firing us with superhuman energy and power. 'Jesus returned in the power of the Spirit,' we read in Luke's description of our Lord's temptation. 'His word was with *power*.' And Jesus himself, after his resurrection, promised the disciples: 'Ye shall receive *power* after that the Holy Spirit is come upon you.'

Thus to visualize the whole picture, we have not only to think of the Spirit slowly, quietly and almost imperceptibly transforming our characters, but also in some cases firing ordinary people with a courage, energy and power far beyond the reach of their natural human capacity. Here we confront the unlimited power which created the world, channelled for its own purposes through the frail vessel of a weak human life. The Spirit, like the wind, 'bloweth where it listeth', and we, poor little ephemeral mortals, cannot tell whence it comes or why it acts thus.

We have to try and appreciate the two-fold truth that, in one sense, the whole world is saturated with and supported by God its Creator. Yet, at the same time, the Spirit enters in a special and entirely personal way into the souls of human beings who abandon themselves entirely to the service and the guidance of God. 'Pour into our hearts such love towards Thee,' we pray—something which is to enter us from outside of ourselves. Yet it is something which finds a ready welcome from the divine seed already dormant within us: 'The Spirit itself beareth witness with our spirit that we are the children of God' (Rom. 8–16).

These facts disprove the suggestion that we are merely the product of evolution, and have produced what laudable qualities we may possess by our own efforts at self-improvement. For however much we try to 'adjust' ourselves to the material world around us, we are still restless and unhappy. For man is both flesh and spirit, and no amount of 'adjustment' to animal life can give him that calm and joy which is the result of developing simultaneously his carnal nature (which is also given to him by God) and his spiritual nature, which is bestowed on him to enable him to reach up out of the material world to union with God.

✠

Here we may ask how man, a half-animal creature at the mercy of circumstance, can become aware of the impalpable existence of the Divine Spirit. We must answer that he cannot do so as a result of his own thoughts or explorations. It is God who acts first, on the condition that we desire him, for our Free Will still enables us to close our minds to him and to occupy ourselves solely with the passing events of daily life. If, however, we want him, he will come. Yet we normally fail completely to visualize the unimaginable glory, splendour and power of the Creator of all the worlds. The vagueness and mystery with which he is surrounded are a merciful provision to spare us. If, therefore, we ask him to come in to us, he will usually do so quietly, gently and gradually, mercifully remembering our weakness. He may well do so in church or through the symbols of religion, which can thus provide a way of entry of the spiritual through the familiar means of material objects.

Those who complain that church services are dull may fail to appreciate that their chief purpose is to provide for us a means by which the Spirit can penetrate into our souls. The corollary of this is that, when the Spirit does enter our souls, it does so unperceived by our conscious intelligence. We were perhaps moved by the outward symbols, but we cannot with our brains appreciate what has happened to us. If we continue to open ourselves to him and to put his service first, our personalities will slowly be changed, unknown to ourselves. Only perhaps after the lapse of years can we remember incidents in our past and realize that, if the same circumstances were to recur now, we should act differently. Our characters have been quietly changed by the indwelling Spirit.

On the other hand, many people are turned to God suddenly and perhaps with strong feelings of emotion. No two people in this world are the same, and we need not be discouraged if our approach to God is different from that of many others. But even those who suddenly become aware of God through a spontaneous conversion, will still pass through the years of quiet, unseen training and moulding by the influence of the Spirit dwelling within. For God knows what is in man and works through his nature in leading him imperceptibly to himself.

✠

Man, in his limited material surroundings, tries to interpret and to classify his experiences according to his own understanding of the material world. Thus, in trying to visualize and 'understand' God, he may picture him as a king seated on a throne with his son sitting on his right hand, sending the Spirit like an agent or messenger to help and encourage their adherents on earth. Such ways of thought are obviously inadequate, helpful though they may be to dear, simple people. So far from merely sending one Spirit, God *is* Spirit, invisible, impalpable and penetrating all creation. It is interesting, however, to notice that the New Testament speaks of indwelling by the Father, by Christ or by the Spirit more or less interchangeably:

> The Father is in me, and I in him.
>
> I speak not of myself, but the Father that dwelleth in me.
>
> I am in my Father, and ye in me, and I in you.
>
> If a man love me, he will keep my words; and my

Father will love him, and we will come unto him and make our abode with him.

The Comforter, which is the Holy Ghost, whom the Father will send in my name.

He that is joined to the Lord is one Spirit.

The Lord is that Spirit: and where the Spirit of the Lord is, there is liberty.

As many as are led by the Spirit of God, they are the sons of God.

Such verses, here collected at random, can be multiplied almost indefinitely from the New Testament.

✠

I cannot avoid the impression that the basis of Christ's revelation to man was that God can dwell inside each one of us, thus placing us in touch with the All-powerful Creator of the Universe. God is Spirit, both outside and inside us, a concept beyond the reach of human reason. Indeed when we consider the frailness and insignificance of man, we appreciate that a god whom we could understand and whose characteristics we could jot down on paper, would be no God at all. Man's little mind, nevertheless, loves to define, to arrange and to classify. He may be helped by visualizing three 'Persons', two of them seated on thrones, for this is picture language which corresponds with something he has seen, and of which he has heard, in human life. But when we observe more carefully the references to the Spirit in the New Testament, we realize that God is one limitless Spirit. It is referred to as 'the Spirit of God'. 'He that is joined to the Lord is one spirit.' 'God sent forth the Spirit of his Son.' 'The supply of the Spirit of Jesus Christ.' 'We have the mind of Christ.' To continue adding to such quotations would be wearisome. Yet they all seem to suggest to me that it is God himself who will dwell in our souls if we invite him.

This is a subject incomprehensible to the finite mind, yet an experience which we can all enjoy. I am amazed at the delicacy of that Providence, which has assisted our feeble and narrow little minds by giving us a human Personality, whom we can clearly visualize, to assist us to give ourselves to an incomprehensible spiritual God.

Come into my heart, Lord Jesus. There is room in my heart for Thee.

St John of the Cross says that every quality produced in men by the Spirit has three distinguishing marks which make it recognizable—tranquillity, gentleness and strength. Our whole outlook on life, our every word and our every action, if we are really filled with the Spirit, must be peaceful, gentle and strong.

I am in no position to air my ideas on so sublime a subject, not being either a theologian or even an intellectual. But most people are neither theologians nor intellectuals, and I am simply one of the common herd. It is as such, that I venture to compare notes with my brothers and sisters. Though it seems to me that a great part of our Lord's teaching was devoted to this doctrine of the Spirit, he also descended to the common level of human thought to explain to us how we should aim to live our lives, once we have decided to give ourselves completely to his service. The following chapters will, therefore, be devoted to the consideration of these more detailed lessons on human life and conduct.

14 *Blueprint for Living*

Before attempting to study the actual teaching of our Lord and how we can deduce from it a model for our own lives, it is necessary to make one important comment. It is that the writings of the first Christians as reported in Acts and in the Epistles, do not represent Christ's teaching as the most important result of his life. They concentrate on the crucifixion and the resurrection as the bases of Christianity.

The crucifixion emphasized the love and the humility of God but, most important of all, the resurrection made possible the hope of life after death. Paul goes so far as to say: 'If Christ be not risen, then is our preaching vain and your faith is also vain.' One might almost go so far as to say that the teachings of Christ became of vital importance to the early Christians, because they were the teachings of him who had risen from the dead. The Orthodox Church has preserved this view of the basic importance of the resurrection better than have the churches of the West. To the former, Easter is the greatest and the most joyful of all the Christian festivals.

Having then emphasized the point that it has always been the resurrection which has been regarded as the seal and the triumph of the life of Christ, let us consider what we may use of his sayings to guide us in our earthly lives.

The teaching of Jesus was extremely simple. Indeed a universal religion must necessarily be so, or the great majority of the human race would be automatically debarred from observing it. To me it seems that his message can be divided into two parts. Firstly, he taught that the sole object of human life was to love God and our fellow men. Secondly, that we cannot do this without God's help but that if we give ourselves entirely and without reserve into his hands, he will spiritually dwell in our souls, and enable us to live the life he enjoins upon us.

This is a summary of our religion—but our Lord illustrated the details of such a life in many lessons and parables, and the next few chapters will be devoted to a closer consideration of these instructions.

The fifth, sixth and seventh chapters of St Matthew's Gospel, commonly called the Sermon on the Mount, provide a basic outline of the new way which Christ brought to the human race. Incidentally, it is significant that to the early Christians their religion was known as *The Way*. In other words, it was not so much a creed as a way of life. Since they had learned this way of living from Christ, it is obvious that they believed in him as divinely inspired. But their belief was simple and uncomplicated. It was only later, with the appearance of an authoritative ecclesiastical hierachy desirous of enforcing discipline, that the emphasis was changed from a way of life to belief in certain statements. Those who had lived the Way became believers.

It is not certain whether the contents of these three chapters of Matthew were originally one sermon, or whether they constitute an epitome of our Lord's teaching. But these sayings are so striking, so original and so typical that they bear the authentic stamp of his thinking.

They begin with the beatitudes—pronouncements of blessedness on certain characteristics attainable by human beings.

I

The first beatitude says: 'Blessed are the poor in spirit; for theirs is the kingdom of heaven.' The expression 'poor in spirit' needs further explanation. A poor-spirited man in today's speech means a man lacking in courage or initiative. J. B. Phillips translates this passage: 'Happy are the humble-minded for the kingdom of heaven is theirs!' The New English Bible says: 'How blest are those who know their need of God; the kingdom of heaven is theirs.'

Humility of spirit seems to be the opposite of the spiritual arrogance of many of the Pharisees and the Sadducees, who considered themselves superior to ordinary people, because they observed the details of the law more precisely. They believed that their own efforts had entitled them to their superiority, and they consequently felt little love or gratitude to God. They had *earned* the right to be leaders by their own efforts. This attitude is the exact opposite to Christ's demand for complete self-donation. Humility is not subservience to other human beings. It is realism—an acknowledgement of our nothingness compared with the immensity, eternity and omniscience of our Creator.

The kingdom of heaven, Christ said elsewhere, is within us. We may thus accept this beatitude to mean, that those who realize their own wretchedness in comparison with the splendour of God, and their impotence without his help, are the people who can live in the Spirit of his kingdom.

II

The second beatitude says: 'Blessed are they that mourn; for they shall be comforted.' J. B. Phillips renders this passage: 'Happy are those who know what sorrow means, for they will be given courage and comfort!' The New

English Bible says: 'How blest are the sorrowful; they shall find consolation.'

It seems to me that this is a warning against frivolity, emphasizing that life is real and earnest, a fact which troubles and reverses enable us to appreciate. It cannot mean that we should go about with dreary expressions on our faces. There are many passages in the New Testament describing the joy and peace experienced by those who follow *The Way*. Moreover the final beatitude tells us to rejoice and be exceeding glad.

If we know that nothing can happen to us in this world contrary to the will of God, we realize that every apparent sorrow and disaster is an exercise set for us by our Teacher. The object is to give us the opportunity to deepen our characters and to learn patience and love. We should welcome every sorrow with quiet joy as a test sent to train us for higher things. Perhaps we may also deduce the conclusion that worldly pleasures and frivolity can absorb our attention, and make us forgetful or even defiant of God. Those who experience sorrows in the world find it easier to remember God, and thus to win that deep, quiet joy, which provides peaceful consolation and independence of the world.

III

The third beatitude reads: 'Blessed are the meek; for they shall inherit the earth.' Here again we are faced with the problem of words which have changed their meaning. Meekness, in modern speech, seems to many people a despicable quality. J. B. Phillips translates this beatitude: 'Happy are those who claim nothing, for the whole earth will belong to them!' The New English Bible says: 'How blest are those of a gentle spirit; they shall have the earth for their possession.' The Jerusalem Bible has: 'Happy the gentle: they shall have the earth for their heritage.' E. V. Rieu's version is almost the same: 'Happy the gentle; for they shall inherit the earth.' Ronald Knox translates it, 'Blessed are the patient; they shall inherit the land.'

I rather like J. B. Phillips' translation. In the world as it is today, we are endlessly obsessed by people claiming their 'rights'. Our world seems to admire the self-assertive who clamour most loudly for their selfish gains. Whether we consider the successful man in big business, or the trade unions demanding more pay, or terrorists or nationalists or imperialists, all are intent only on fighting their fellow mortals in order to obtain more benefits for themselves at somebody else's expense.

We moan and lament at the chaotic state of the world which is produced precisely by the narrow selfishness of our own outlook. How happy indeed should we be if more of us made no selfish claims, but realized that it is indeed more blessed to give than to receive, a phrase which is repeated in several places in the New Testament. Perhaps these ten words go as near as any to summarize the gospel of Christ. This short phrase is truly revolutionary when compared to the standards of the world, which normally aim at gain or profit—that is to say to receive more than they give.

A learned friend of mine informs me that the Greek word translated as 'meek' in Matthew 5.5, was originally used of a fiery war horse which had been perfectly broken in and schooled, so as to be always immediately responsive to his master's every touch, or signal, without losing any of his own high spirit or courage. I cannot comment on this interpretation for I have never learned Greek. But the comparison certainly seems extremely apt, for the Christian must indeed be at all times perfectly sensitive to every indication of God's will, but without losing any of his own energy, initiative or courage. Such an interpretation avoids the modern implications of meek as being submissive and compliant.

IV

'Blessed are they which do hunger and thirst after righteousness; for they shall be filled.' This passage is very similar in J. B. Phillips' version except that he changes 'righteousness' into the more modern word 'goodness'. Ronald Knox translates the same word as 'holiness'. The Jerusalem Bible speaks of 'those who hunger and thirst for what is right'.

It seems to me that this beatitude emphasizes the necessity for the complete dedication of our lives. Our passionate longing for God is likened to hunger and thirst. In his *Readings in St John's Gospel*, Archbishop Temple says that there are not sins, but one sin. 'There is only one sin, and it is characteristic of the whole world. It is the self-will which prefers *my* way to God's—which puts *me* in the centre where only God is in place.' To hunger and thirst after goodness is the opposite of devoting all our efforts to our own advantage.

V

'Blessed are the merciful; for they shall obtain mercy,' seems to require no comment.

VI

'Blessed are the pure in heart; for they shall see God.' J. B. Phillips translates this, 'Happy are the utterly sincere, for they will see God!' Other translators all seem to retain 'pure in heart'. Purity of heart seems to me the opposite of that quality of sophistication which is so much sought after nowadays. To be pure in heart is to see only the best in other people, which often results in drawing the best out of them. It is the quality of simplicity, which we find so attractive in country people, or in those 'backward' populations, who welcome all comers into their homes with smiles.

Purity of heart is the quality contrasting with the attitude of those people who are determined never to be caught off their guard, and who suspect everyone else of being deceivers or of having an ulterior motive. Purity of heart is perhaps the product of the purity of our own intentions, the direct opposite of cynicism about human nature.

It is interesting to notice that the reward of purity of heart is to be able to *see* God. If we believe that every human being has a seed of divinity implanted in his or her soul, our readiness to believe in other people enables us to see God in them. Many saints have said that they saw Christ in every individual whom they encountered.

VII

'Blessed are the peacemakers; for they shall be called the children of God.' J. B. Phillips renders this beatitude: 'Happy are those who make peace, for they will be known as sons of God!' The New English Bible version reads: 'How blest are the peacemakers; God shall call them His sons.'

Peace-making seems to be one of the virtues furthest from our restless, grabbing age. We do not of course wish for war, and we direct our most acid criticisms against those who, we believe, were responsible for the wars of the past. But our whole way of life is an active incentive to war. The mentality which sees the accumulation of wealth as the object of life inevitably leads to a clash with others similarly minded. The same applies to industrial peace, continually broken by clashes between groups both of which are animated by a desire for more money, regardless of the interests of their fellow citizens who constitute the nation. Sometimes even, these confrontations seem to be solely inspired by a spirit of bellicosity which is spoiling for a fight and which, like all wars, can only lead to the impoverishment and ruin of both sides.

These examples are obvious, but the damage done to peace by writing and by speech is not so fully realized. This seems to me to apply especially to the press, which never ceases to pour its contempt on other countries. Only people who have lived for many years abroad appreciate the intensity of the resentments produced in other countries by the scornful remarks about them which appear continually in the British press. The newspapers claim to be the guardians of our liberties, but they are also one of the chief producers of national hatreds.

VIII

'Blessed are they which are persecuted for righteousness' sake; for theirs is the kingdom of heaven.' Nearly all the translators seem to agree on this wording. J. B. Phillips says, 'Happy are those who have suffered persecution for the cause of goodness ...' The next two verses further elaborate the same theme.

'Blessed are ye, when men shall revile you and persecute you, and shall say all manner of evil against you falsely, for my sake. Rejoice and be exceeding glad, for great is your reward in heaven.' The fact of being abused and persecuted does not perhaps seem to us blessed, but the persecution is said to be the result of our goodness. If the kingdom of heaven is within us, it will control our lives, if we are so dedicated to service that we can face persecution. Indeed it is only God within us, who can give us the strength to endure persecution with joy.

If we briefly summarize these eight aphorisms, we find the following qualities to be recommended.

(*a*) The recognition of our own nothingness compared with the omnipotence and the eternity of the Creator.

(*b*) The need to take life seriously, as against the world's pursuit of frivolity and pleasure, it being understood that our sobriety can bring us a quiet joy and peace.

(*c*) The necessity to avoid claimfulness for ourselves, remembering that the sin of sins is self-preoccupation.

(*d*) To dedicate ourselves body and soul to the love and service of God and our fellow men.

(*e*) To show mercy to all the world as far as lies in us. Perhaps mercy needs to take the initiative more often and not to wait until some living thing is at our mercy.

(*f*) Purity of heart—to see the best in everybody we meet. Every such encounter is a joyful opportunity to show love.

(*g*) To devote ourselves everywhere to sow peace in place of discord. This injunction not only prohibits us from the actual use of war, violence or coercion. It also forbids violence in speech or criticism, or the expression of hatred or resentment which leads to breaches of the peace.

(*h*) Finally such utter dedication to the service of God and humanity that we are prepared to endure ostracism, physical persecution or even death.

The principal quality required in this outline character sketch is selfless dedication. But I cannot avoid the impression of quietness and serenity which seems to permeate the whole picture. 'The servant of the Lord must not strive,' wrote Paul to Timothy, 'but be gentle unto all men.' We see thus an outline sketch of a man or a woman who, before all else, is conscious of his or her own nothingness before God, but who is utterly dedicated to selfless service. The whole picture is calm, in contrast to the clamour, noise and turmoil of modern life.

The third chapter of Paul's second letter to Timothy may perhaps, in contrast, sound more familiar to us. 'This know also,' he writes, 'that in the last days perilous times shall come. For men shall be lovers of their own selves, covetous, boasters, proud, blasphemers, disobedient to parents, unthankful, unholy, without natural affection, truce breakers, false accusers, incontinent, fierce, despisers of those that are good, traitors, heady, high-minded, lovers of pleasure more than lovers of God.' I found it interesting this morning to check through this list after reading the morning newspaper, and to notice how many of these peculiarities seem to be apparent in our modern society!

✠

The effect produced by the beatitudes is one of quiet, peace, modesty, dedication, calm courage and faithfulness to death. It is noticeable that these are all interior states. There is no mention of external actions, the importance of going to church, collecting money, working hard or the fulfilment of routine duties. Doubtless the beatitudes are the firm foundations of the Christian life, for all external actions find their origin in our interior spiritual state. Our thoughts are the mainspring of our actions.

Christians, it has been said, may be divided into the interior and the exterior variety. Interior Christians are those who endeavour to form their characters on the beatitudes and, after laying this foundation, set out to serve God and the world in their activities. Exterior Christians throw themselves into external activities to benefit others, or perhaps into the exact observance of outward religious duties, such as church attendance or the giving of money. Not having first laid the foundations, they may be touchy, quarrelsome or impatient, or show other defects of character. In spite of the practical value of their services, they dim the radiance of the Christian life. To outsiders, their energetic activity in Church work proves them indisputably to be Christians, but their ill-temper or their sharp tongues discredit the Christian character. Like the Pharisees, their intentions may be good but they repel the layman from joining them. Thus we see that our Lord commences with the beatitudes, and from them he goes on to particularize. Let us then endeavour to lay a blessed foundation before seeking too rapidly to erect an outward edifice.

It is not necessary to draw too hard and fast a line between interior and exterior Christians. Sometimes perhaps exterior activities directed to serving others may lead to interior progress. But our interior state is ultimately the touchstone of our lives. Put in another way, we may perhaps say that the secret of blessedness lies in our motivation—to serve God and our fellow human beings in completely selfless dedication or, in other words, to lead an interior not an exterior life.

The ten commandments delivered to Moses related largely, though not entirely, to actions—murder, theft, adultery. Our Lord said that he had not come to destroy the Law but to fulfil it—to carry it a step nearer to perfection. This fulfilment consisted in developing it from exterior actions to interior motivation. The prohibition of murder was developed into a prohibition of hatred or contempt. Even to call one's brother a fool became an offence. The prohibition against the outward act of theft was extended to one forbidding us to devote our lives to the accumulation of money or of worldly treasures upon earth. If our only motive is selfless service to God and man our actions will automatically harmonize with our inner self-surrender.

15 *The Way*

At the end of the beatitudes are included a number of comments intended to fill out the picture of *The Way*. The new Way of life was a complete reversal of the popular ideas of the time, as indeed it is of the standards of our world today. The world admires the successful man who has spent his life in accumulating money, which he will leave behind when he dies. It sympathizes with the good fighter who has stood up for his 'rights', that is to say, he has put himself first and has done his best to suppress all rivals.

This self-centred way of living is diametrically opposed to the new Way, in which a man is not to think of himself, but to spend his life in loving, helping, and serving other people. It is a turn round through a hundred and eighty degrees, to go in exactly the opposite direction. Comparatively few people, Christ said, will find this narrow way, so we need not be discouraged at the state of the world, for he foresaw that the majority of people would follow the broad way leading to destruction.

We may ask what becomes of the majority of the human race who follow the broad way, but this we are not told. If God were to issue a brochure in advance, describing the joys of heaven and the terrors of destruction, more men might choose the narrow way. But their choice would not be inspired by love and devotion but would be aimed to secure the best conditions when they retired from life. Their decisions would be guided by selfish motives. Moral decisions *must* be taken for love or duty, not with an eye to ultimate gain. To preserve the value of our decisions, we must be kept in ignorance of our ultimate future. The numbers of people who follow this narrow way being so small, they run the risk of being conspicuous. But although the majority of the human race will not follow them, yet their example will serve to influence the whole of society. They can be compared to a candle which gives light to all in the house—or to salt, a tiny powdery sprinkling, which adds flavour to the whole stew.

Our Lord explained that he had not come to act against the Law, but he pointed out that laws, enforced by the authorities, are exterior to people. They may obey them from fear of punishment rather than for moral reasons. The origin of crime is in human thought. The prevention of crime, therefore, depends on the purification of our thoughts. There is therefore little use in increasing the penalties for crime, assault, murder or terrorism. The only positive cure is the spread of love, and the reduction of hate, jealousy and resentment. In the same way, the only method of avoiding sexual immorality is to banish lustful thoughts from our minds. This can often be done by the offering up of a quick prayer and by turning to another occupation. We must beware that we do not really half-encourage our thoughts of lust or resentment. God cannot be deceived. He will not remove them if we ourselves are secretly encouraging them.

Under the old dispensation, our Lord continued, it was thought right to love your friends but to hate your enemies. Regarding the latter, the law of revenge was observed, 'an eye for an eye and a tooth for a tooth'. Perhaps in the Western world we no longer apply quite so crude a code, yet revenge is a subject often referred to in books or on the television.

Though we may not all seek to revenge ourselves

physically on personal enemies, in the world of nationalism vengeance is still carried to absurd lengths. Alleged injuries inflicted on one nation by another hundreds, or even thousands, of years ago, must today be 'avenged' with the pistol, the machine-gun or the time bomb, if not by open war. Often the national name may have survived, but the ethnic composition of the people has completely changed. Any injuries inflicted have long since ceased. Yet acts of 'revenge' of this kind are actually commended, or at least not denounced, even by persons who call themselves Christians.

But the words of Christ are crystal clear. 'Love your enemies, bless them that curse you, do good to them that hate you, and pray for them which despitefully use you and persecute you.' It may be noted that the command to love applies to persons who are actually cursing, hating and ill-using us NOW. How much more would they apply to another nation which is no longer ill-treating us, and any grievance against which has long ago ceased.

Quite apart from any religious feeling, it is obvious to most of us that violence leads only to more violence. Yet newspapers report that the World Council of Churches has given money to African nationalists engaged in terrorist acts. Is it possible that the members of the World Council of Churches have never read the fifth chapter of St Matthew's gospel? How can people calling themselves Christians support actions so utterly and diametrically opposed to the teachings of Christ?

In fact, however, the contrast is even more striking than a mere neglect of our Lord's command to love our enemies. For during his lifetime, the situation in Palestine was almost exactly the same as that of which nationalists complain today. Palestine was administered by the Romans, taxation was onerous and the government was corrupt. Jewish zealots constantly attempted to draw our Lord into violent rebellion, a situation which caused him frequent difficulties. Yet he never agreed for one moment to countenance the use of violence. It does not seem to me possible under any circumstances whatever, for serious Christians to extenuate—much less to encourage—the use of violence in politics.

Jewish extremism in Palestine at the time of our Lord, resulted ultimately in the destruction of Jerusalem by Titus. How much happier would have been the fate of the Jews if they had eschewed violence. Let us, at least, be perfectly clear in our minds that sincere Christians can never extenuate the use of violence for aggression or revenge. (The question of defence is dealt with in a later chapter.)

The last verse of the fifth chapter of Matthew's gospel reads, 'Be ye therefore perfect, even as your Father which is in heaven is perfect'. For God maintains a calm, gentle and benevolent attitude to all, and sends rain alike on the just and on the unjust. So also must we be calm and gentle, wishing well to all men. For every human being is an individual soul. There can never be any justification for communal and national hatreds, nor for venting hate and revenge on an individual because he or she belongs to any race or party.

The nineteenth to the twenty-fourth verse of the sixth chapter of Matthew contains the well-known prohibition against laying up for ourselves treasures upon earth. The reason why the accumulation of wealth is forbidden is because where our treasure is, there will our hearts be also. If we dedicate our lives to the accumulation of money, our thoughts will be absorbed in doing so. We cannot at the same time devote ourselves to the service of God and also to the making of money. We all know by experience how true this is. If we devote ourselves to amassing riches, we have little time to relax or to think of anything else.

But it is worth while to emphasize that the mistake lies in the fact that money so easily monopolizes our thoughts. It is not that money in itself is evil, nor the worldly benefits which money can bring, provided that the service of God is first in our thoughts. Obviously, if this is the case, we shall not be miserly in the use of our money. The evil is to allow anything at all to fill our minds to the exclusion of God. I do not think that any of the blessings of life are evil, if we accept them as gifts from God, and give him precedence in our minds, even while we are enjoying them.

Certain processes are necessary to the continued existence of the human race. God in his mercy has facilitated these processes by making them pleasant. We are obliged to eat. If all food were like cotton wool, how wearisome it would be to take nourishment. But the Father in his mercy has provided for this problem by making food taste good. In the same way we need to drink, and the process of drinking when we are thirsty is enjoyable. The union of a man and a woman is necessary for the propagation of the human race and, as a result, God has made it pleasurable. If it were not so, who would undertake the responsibility of producing a family? The more aesthetic pleasures of life—art, music, poetry, literature and the beauties of nature—are all likewise gifts of God to make our earthly pilgrimage more pleasant, but all are governed by the same condition—they must not fill our minds to the exclusion of our Father.

✠

In studying the details of our Lord's teaching, which follows the beatitudes, we have given precedence to the two most obvious problems of the Western world today—violence and the love of money. He told us with perfect frankness that we must love our enemies, even while they are still persecuting us. How right he was in saying that those who take the sword will perish by the sword. We realize the suicidal results of violence when we contemplate all the bitter little wars which are being fought in the world today, the heartbreaking sufferings of the refugees driven from their homes, and the ruin and desolation of their countries.

His condemnation of the spirit of intransigence and revenge was emphasized by the fact that he depicted God's forgiveness of our trespasses as conditional on our forgiveness of those who sinned against us. How, in the face of these repeated statements, can any sincere Christian advocate the use of violence, or justify revenge, even against former aggressors.

Christ's prohibition of the accumulation of wealth is equally emphatic. The passion for money is so engrossing, he explained, that it absorbs all our thoughts and makes it impossible for us to think of God. 'You cannot *serve* God and money,' he said. To serve money means that we allow money to become our master. As long as money is only a means of exchange in our service, it enables us to use those gifts which God has given us to make our earthly stay more useful and pleasurable. But it is no exaggeration to say that in the Western world today money is the master of most of our lives and from it we seek to attain power over our fellow human-beings, not to share with them the merciful gifts of God.

16 *Judge Not*

In considering the detailed lessons given by our Lord in illustration of the beatitudes, we have noticed his condemnation of hatred and violence, and his prohibition of making the accumulation of wealth the object of our lives. A further lesson is founded in the seventh chapter of St Matthew's gospel which begins with the passage: 'Judge not, that ye be not judged. For with what judgement ye judge, ye shall be judged; and with what measure ye mete, it shall be measured to you again. And why beholdest thou the mote that is in thy brother's eye, but considerest not the beam that is in thine own eye.' The New English Bible says: 'Why do you look at the speck of sawdust in your brother's eye, with never a thought for the great plank in your own.'

How few of us pay even the slightest attention to this perfectly plain command given by our Lord. Perhaps our most obvious breach of his order is in our personal affairs. Even coming out of church, when our minds should be filled with warm, human love, we begin to criticize the sermon or the way in which the service has been conducted.

How unkind we are in speaking of our neighbours and of the people we meet every day. Nothing abusive perhaps—just a little drop of poison now and again, a malicious innuendo or a witty sarcasm. These are not mere slips of the tongue. For Christ himself said that it is 'out of the abundance of the heart the mouth speaketh'. A good man produces good words from his own store of goodness, a bad man draws spiteful words from his own jealous and malicious thoughts. 'But I say unto you, that every idle word that men shall speak, they shall give account thereof in the day of judgement. For by thy words thou shalt be justified, and by thy words thou shalt be condemned.' (Matthew 12.34–7)

How many of us have ever pondered this terrifying statement? We shall be called to give account for every idle word. How many idle, careless, spiteful words do we pronounce every day! It is not enough to abstain from theft, murder or adultery. We shall be called to account for every little casual spiteful remark. These unkind words which we throw off so carelessly may seem to us unimportant, but they are revelations of the jealousy, malice and vanity of our minds. We like secretly to think of ourselves as better than all these other people. Thus we take a jealous pleasure in finding fault with them, in order to prove our superiority.

How very, very far are these jealousies from that love which is God himself. Why cannot we restrain our tongues from making derogatory remarks? The answer is, as Christ emphasizes so forcibly, that we cannot do so as long as we nurse jealousy and malice in our minds. Just as lustful thoughts result in adultery, so jealous thoughts produce spiteful words. We cannot control the words which come out, if our thoughts are not truly loving. The only cure for this fault which Christ denounced so sternly is in the gradual process of uprooting vanity and self-preoccupation from our hearts, and filling them with a general benevolence towards all mankind. This is beyond our power unless the Spirit dwells in our souls.

✠

So much for the petty jealousy and unkindness of our thoughts, a feature of human nature which seems to date from time immemorial. But in a wider field, criticism seems to be a peculiar fault of our times. Our general malevolence seems to colour our whole attitude to the world. Perhaps the endless stream of fault-finding which we direct at the whole world is the result of the wide extension of cynicism throughout the West. The pure in heart see the best in everybody. In the beatitudes we were told that they see God. Not only do they see him working in the world, directing all things in wisdom, but they see him in all the people they meet or of whom they hear. They know that a divine seed exists in every human soul, if only it can be allowed to work. In every human being, they rejoice to see a potential Christ. This general benevolence enables them to see the best side in everyone.

The weakening of Christian love in many people, and perhaps most of all in the media of public information, has reduced the number of the pure in heart—or at least has made it more difficult to hear their voices. The atmosphere of cynicism, spite and ill-will reflected in the newspapers has infected all our minds.

I do not think that this has always been the case. In reading the books and letters of an earlier age, we find frequent expressions of loyalty and affection for others, even for persons in high office. In the Western nations today, however, a new head of state or prime minister may be welcomed when he assumes office. But very soon the tune changes and torrents of criticism, abuse and innuendo are directed against him. Persons who hold high public office are subjected to very great strain from the complications of our industrial society, the importance of the decisions which they must take, their long hours of work and their frequent engagements. On top of all this, the vilification which they suffer makes their burdens almost unbearable. Such an atmosphere seems, moreover, to deter men of honour and sensitivity from engaging in politics. The very men and women whom we need in public office, the dedicated, the broad-minded, those who are enthusiastic to render service—these people are deterred from engaging in what many people regard as an unsavoury profession. The debates in the House of Commons do little to dispel such an impression.

It is a law of human nature that we respond to the treatment which we receive. If we feel ourselves trusted, we become trustworthy. If we are regarded with suspicion, our conduct will probably be tortuous. If we feel ourselves to be loved, we tend to return that love. If we despise the people by whom we are ruled, is that situation partly due to ourselves and to the manner in which we treat our rulers?

The ideal of government in all ages and in all nations, is that of power directed by love, and thereby calling out the love of the governed. I have personally seen this system in action, here and there in various countries, and I am perfectly convinced that it is a practicable ideal, at least to a considerable extent. The government, whatever its superficial form, must possess power, for there are always criminals and delinquents, even if only a few. But if those in authority are felt to love the people, the vast majority of the governed will give love in return. In such an atmosphere, crime will dwindle to a negligible quantity for the people will be active supporters of the authority.

But it is no use laying all the blame on the poor quality of our politicians. If it takes two to make a quarrel, it also takes two to make co-operation. Perhaps the party system is to some degree responsible. The mutual criticisms of the politicians and of the members of the public are more often than not inspired by party interests. In so far as we, the general public, are concerned, however, let us remember Christ's prohibition against judging others, whether they be those in public office or the neighbours in our own street. We shall be judged for every idle, spiteful word which we utter.

The universal habit of spiteful criticism is perhaps partly due to the modern misuse of the word 'equality'. Christianity tells us that all men are equal before God—that is to say that he loves all his creatures. All citizens must obviously be equal before the law, which means that neither wealth nor intellectual superiority should give an advantage in legal proceedings. In most ways, however, men and women are by no means equal. Indeed it is one of the miracles of creation that no two people in the world are exactly the same. Some are born more intelligent than others, some physically stronger. More important still, some people are more energetic and industrious than others, some of higher moral character, some of more violent temper, some more patient and courteous, some more cheerful or more affectionate.

These inborn, hereditary differences, which none of us can alter, are further accentuated by the upbringing of children. I do not refer to the differences produced by wealth or social status, but to the varying characters of parents. Some fathers and mothers are kind, patient, wise and conscientious, some are ill-tempered, violent, drunken, or too pre-occupied with their own business or pleasure to give adequate time and affection to their children. Thus men and women, by the time they have grown up, vary immensely in every possible respect, in intelligence, in education, in physical strength, in energy and diligence, and in moral character, honesty, kindness, love and a sense of duty.

In the ideal society every man should be able to find his way to the employment for which he is most suited, not only in intelligence or physical strength, but in view of his moral qualities, his honesty, truthfulness and sense of duty. Especially should senior positions be awarded to the most efficient, on condition that they are also the most honest, the most diligent and those of the highest moral character.

The conclusion is that, in most respects, men and

women differ to an almost unbelievable degree, in capability and in moral qualities. The illogical trend in much modern thought is to claim that all men and women are equal, not only before God and the law, but in every other respect. This utterly unrealistic tendency destroys all respect for authority. The people at the bottom think themselves equal to the people at the top. Perhaps the point could be better illustrated by saying that all people are equal, but all are not the same. Some are better organizers than others and should be placed in charge of organizational work, those less skilled being placed under their orders. Those with a genius for figures should be made chief accountants while others less gifted are subordinate to them, and so on.

There are in our society many people of high moral character and devotion to their work, but, according to the muddled thinking of our time, to show respect for such would suggest that we are not 'equal' to them. To admit that anyone else is entitled to a higher salary than I am is to admit our inequality. To be more industrious, more skilled or more intelligent than I am is offensive. Such a person probably thinks that I am not his 'equal'.

It is obvious that no community or organization can survive unless there be senior people in control, who make plans and give orders. The distortion of equality to mean that the authorities need not be obeyed, but can be vilified by all with impunity, can only result in confusion and collapse.

In the days when children were taught the catechism, they learned that it was incumbent on them 'to do their duty in that state of life into which it shall please God to call them'. I do not think that this phrase prevented anyone from trying to rise in life, as is shown by the immense energy displayed by the Victorians, but they realized that the way to get on was to acquire the necessary qualities of skill, diligence and honesty. The distortion of equality which causes people at the bottom to claim that they are 'equal' to those at the top, without acquiring the necessary qualities, must inevitably lead to insubordination and chaos.

✠

Perhaps the issue can be put in another way. It is obviously in the interest of the community and the nation that the 'best' people, morally and intellectually, should rise to the top. Freedom of opportunity should be our aim, on condition that moral as well as intellectual qualities are taken into consideration. But if our basic principle is that everybody must be equal, there is no way of achieving it except by preventing the most capable and the most deserving from reaching the top positions, whether by laws discriminating against them or by unofficial means. The issue is therefore plain. Freedom of opportunity should enable the best to reach the most responsible posts and is therefore in the best interests of the country. Measures to prevent the best reaching the top, in the supposed interests of equality, are disastrous for the country.

It is extraordinary how often we find that the more careful observance of one of our Lord's prohibitions would have enabled us to avoid an immense area of the confusion and muddled thinking which is reducing society to chaos. I believe that his words, 'judge not that ye be not judged,' are a case in point. How much happier our lives would be if we behaved with more affection and tolerance towards our neighbours. How much more prosperous and contented our nation would be if we first removed the planks from our own eyes, instead of expending so much spite and malevolence in denouncing the specks of dust in everyone else's eyes. How often a few words in the gospels are sufficient to clear up a vast area of confusion in our minds.

17 *Unconditional Surrender*

We have seen in the previous chapter that Christ warned us against judging and criticizing other people, a prohibition which seems to be generally disregarded nowadays. But he did not limit his commands to the words we say or write—he applied them also to action. In the sixth chapter of St Luke there is another version of the beatitudes. In verse 29 we read, 'Unto him that smiteth thee on the one cheek offer also the other: and him that taketh away thy cloak forbid not to take thy coat also.'

Many people regard these commands as absurd. If you offer the other cheek, they say, he will hit you again, and finally, he will knock you down and kill you. If anyone hits you, the only course is to hit back even harder. This seemingly obvious reaction overlooks a number of relevant factors, of which perhaps the most important is that divine seed which lies buried in every human soul, and which can be fired by courage and by love.

In considering the parable of striking the cheek, the essential factor is not to hit back, but not to run away. To hit back merely adds to the hatred and the violence in the world. But it is essential to be fearless, to stand up to the aggressor in quiet calm. Such actions will often change the attacker himself.

I first encountered a situation of this kind forty-five years ago when I was serving an Arab state. Raiding and fighting had been going on for many years between the subjects of the government which I was serving and one of its neighbours. A conference had recently been held between delegations from the two governments under

British mediation. Both sides had presented extravagant claims for compensation, high words had been exchanged, and the conference broke up with increasingly exacerbated feelings.

Shortly afterwards I was placed in charge of the disturbed frontier as a servant of one of the governments concerned, and a meeting was arranged between the representative of the other government and myself. He arrived with long lists of claims. I had not really thought out the problem, but something moved me to say, 'I don't know how we can ever sort out all these claims, but I know your Excellency to be a man of honour—I don't want to argue but I am prepared to accept in advance any solution which you think is just.' His attitude changed in an instant. 'I could not possibly do that,' he said. '*You* must decide what is right.' In a minute we were both arguing that the other must decide unilaterally. In a short time, we reached a solution, each of us vying to give way to the other. We became close personal friends and from that moment raiding ceased on that previously turbulent frontier. This is a small example but it impressed me with the falsity of the conception that one can get nothing in this world without fighting for it.

In fact, love evokes love, toleration brings out toleration and honesty calls out the honesty of an opponent. This was not a trick to deceive the other party by guile. But good intentions can be transparent and evoke a surprising response. It is on some such principles that I interpret the parable of turning the other cheek. Stand up to an aggressor but do not hit back.

This is only a small practical example to illustrate how often fighting is unnecessary. But as Christians we have to look deeper. The background of our lives should be that nothing can happen to us without God's consent. If, therefore, something unpleasant occurs, we know that God has permitted it in order to teach us a needful lesson.

As a result, if we complain or grumble, we must realize that we are rebelling against God.

We cannot present him with a written list of claims, so we resort to self-pity and bemoan our fate. But we can say to him: 'I cannot overcome my troubles through my own strength. Do you settle it all, my Lord, for I know that you love me.' As soon as we sincerely offer this prayer, our burden is lightened. The essential is always to remember that everything which happens to us in this life is sent by God for our own improvement and to enable us to help other people. To complain, to grumble, or to indulge in self-pity is rebellion against God. Neither is there any need to be afraid, for if he sends the trial, he will also supply the strength to overcome it. 'I can do *all* things through Christ which strengtheneth me,' wrote Paul to the Philippians. Nothing, I repeat, nothing could overwhelm us or conquer us in this life, if we relied completely and utterly on God's strength.

But there is a further stage of progress which we must achieve. Many Christians succeed, more or less, in resigning themselves to what they believe is God's will. With heroic patience, they endure their misery or their suffering, repeating to themselves, 'God's will be done.' When we really believe, however, that God sends us our troubles to enable us to learn and to progress, we see that mere resignation is not free from self-pity. If we were really surrendered to him, and if we truly believed that everything that happens to us comes from him, we should be *glad* to receive whatever he sends. 'If you are not glad, then you are complaining,' writes Merlin Carothers, and complaining is rebellion against God.

These considerations also affect our relations with other people. Paul connected the two subjects together. In Ephesians 5.20–1, he writes, 'Giving thanks always for all things unto God and the Father in the name of our Lord Jesus Christ, submitting yourselves one to another in the fear of God.' When we realize that it is God who sends the difficult boss, the irritable colleague or the aggressive heckler, we can rejoice to submit to his will and to our troublesome neighbour. Then your relaxed, calm and good-natured answer will turn away wrath.

All our difficulties with people are a three-cornered relationship. Our first and continual task is to be completely surrendered to God and always to think of him first. When we become involved in a difficulty with another human being, our first task is to look quickly to God, to thank him for the situation which he has sent and to beg him to guide us through it. Then we can turn to the other person, our souls full of gladness and love.

In the preceding chapter, we considered our habit of continual criticism, of the other members of our families, of our neighbours, of those in public office or of everyone else of whom we read or hear. Even the weather is the endless object of our complaints and grumbles. But we are now considering not so much words as actions. Revolt is criticism carried into action. One of the most striking characteristics of our times is indiscipline—the refusal to submit to one another.

Perhaps this situation is partly due to mistakes in the upbringing of children, who are encouraged to 'develop their own personalities' by doing whatever they feel inclined. 'Discipline in schools has been superseded,' a school teacher recently informed me. True discipline is not arbitrary compulsion. It is the ingrained habit of service, of forgetting ourselves to serve the common good. It must surely be a catastrophic error to encourage children to do as they feel inclined, and thus to represent selfishness as an admirable quality.

The effect is everywhere visible in our society—'I want to do my own thing,' 'I couldn't care less,' 'Why should I?' are typical phrases. Surely the foundation of all education should be to inculcate into the child the fact that we are all born to serve. The greatest of us, our Lord said, should be the servant of all. The only persons we should never consider are ourselves. Discipline is selflessness erected into a system; it is not subjection to arbitrary tyranny enforced by fear.

Every order, rule or regulation must be laid down on this basis. When I was an army officer, my subordinates were sometimes brought up for trial on disciplinary charges, such as neglecting to obey an order. I always endeavoured to explain to the accused the reason for discipline, which is not an arbitrary system imposed on its victims by compulsion. Discipline is a voluntary association for the common good. I would explain to the man that the unit to which we both belonged was responsible for certain duties, which senior commanders relied upon it to perform. The whole army is a closely integrated service, in which everyone relies on everybody else to do his part. If people here and there neglect their duties, the whole organization is thrown into confusion. It is, therefore, essential that each one of us realize our obligation and voluntarily bind ourselves to serve together.

An army is a nation in miniature. The prosperity of the whole depends on the voluntary service of every member of the community. To make the rebel into a hero is to destroy the peace of the whole nation and to frustrate its hopes for the future. Nothing can be achieved by an organization constantly divided against itself.

In order to encourage rebellion, a vague and imaginary entity has been created called the 'establishment', against which we are encouraged to fight. In fact, no such enemy exists. Discipline is voluntary co-operation. He that would be first among us must be the servant of all. Both top people and junior people often fail in their service and have to be brought back into co-operation by the patient assistance of their neighbours or colleagues.

18 *Of Human Suffering*

In considering the world of our hearts' desire in Chapter 5, we found that we could not imagine a world without suffering. We also concluded that the greater part of human suffering is inflicted by human beings on one another, though some forms of suffering, such as bereavement, natural disasters and certain diseases are not caused by other people. We also discovered that a world without pain or suffering would be a world without heroism and without most of the compassion, sympathy and devotion which call forth the best in human nature. In the present chapter, we shall consider especially the effect of suffering on the sufferer.

'How can there be a God of Love when we see so much suffering in the world?' is a question we often hear asked today. I do not personally see any great problem in this question for the following reasons:

1. I commence by re-iterating the assumption which we have already made, namely, that God exists and that he desires to raise us (perhaps originally from an animal condition) to a moral status enabling us to communicate with him, presumably for ever.

2. When we consider the animal world and the human race as it is today, we can vaguely realize what an immense task this seems to be, at any rate to our tiny minds. God is the Creator of the universe, a phrase the realization of which needs a great deal of thought in order to penetrate our minds. If God is pure goodness, man has been described as fallen, evil and desperately wicked. Yet Christ said that we must be perfect like God himself. To our

limited minds, such a task seems well-nigh impossible, though with God all things are possible. At any rate, we can appreciate its difficulty.

3. The statement that a God of Love would not allow anyone to suffer must be considered in the light of the problem of how to make us all perfect. Perhaps we should consider what we mean by love. It seems to suggest to some people a sentimental kindness which cannot bear to see a baby crying. Give him a lolly, even if it will spoil his next meal. How lovely to see him smile again. This is a sort of senile grandfather kindness to which the parents often object!

4. If then we consider the present moral state of mankind and the fact that the target is a perfection which would enable us to communicate with God, we begin to realize that this object cannot be achieved by merely ensuring that everyone always has a nice time. A great deal of discipline, testing and even punishment will be needed.

5. In Hebrews 12.5–8, we read:

> My son despise not thou the chastening of the Lord, nor faint when thou art rebuked of him: for whom the Lord loveth he chasteneth, and scourgeth every son whom he receiveth. If ye endure chastening, God dealeth with you as with sons; for what son is he whom the father chasteneth not? But if ye be without chastisement, whereof all are partakers, then are ye bastards, and not sons.

In ancient times, the head of a great house might have many sons by concubines. Nice little boys with whom their father would enjoy playing and seeing them happy. Their future did not much matter. But his son by his wife would be a different matter. He would one day be head of the family and the honour of the family name would rest on him. No trouble would be too great to train and discipline him. He would be educated by a severe tutor, be made to undergo tests of endurance and danger, be taught courtesy and consideration for others. Whether he liked it or not, he must be subjected to obedience and hardship to ensure that one day he would prove himself a worthy leader.

6. Even in our own limited experience of life, we know that when all goes easily and we are young, healthy and have plenty of money, we pass our time all too easily in pleasure and frivolity. But when we suddenly experience a disaster, an agonizing bereavement, the loss of a promising career, we change our outlook. We fall on our knees and ask God to save us. 'It is good for me that I have been afflicted that I might learn Thy statutes,' admitted the psalmist some three thousand years ago.

7. It is perhaps unnecessary to labour the point much further. If we consider the matter seriously, we can imagine what sort of human race would result if God's 'love' showed itself by making sure that we always had a nice time and lots of fun. ''Tis the hard grey weather breeds hard Englishmen,' sang Charles Kingsley.

8. It must be admitted that the decadent atmosphere of Britain today may be chiefly responsible for the plea that if God loved us, he would arrange for us all to have a nice time. For in recent years, we have been assured that parents should not try to discipline their children. The ever lengthening lists of juvenile criminals and social drop-outs are a sufficient commentary. Almost every other consideration should be subordinated to the inculcation of duty and of selflessness.

9. I was recently reading a Christian pamphlet written some twenty years ago, which referred to suffering as a strange and incomprehensible part of our world, and

added that there exists 'the problem of the presence in human life of an inescapable core of innocent and, as far as we can see, unnecessary suffering'. The use of the word innocent is noticeable, and seems to be a hark-back to the pre-Christian belief that suffering was a punishment which God inflicted upon us for our sins. The author of the Epistle to the Hebrews knew better, for he says 'whom the Lord loveth he chasteneth'.

10. Throughout the Old Testament, the belief is expressed that suffering in this life is a punishment inflicted on the wicked and that the righteous should be always happy and successful. Psalm 91 is one of the best known of such passages and says in part:

> I will say of the Lord, He is my refuge ... Thou shalt not be afraid for the terror by night; nor for the arrow that flieth by day. Nor for the pestilence that walketh in darkness ... A thousand shall fall at thy side and ten thousand at thy right hand; but it shall not come nigh thee. Only with thine eyes shalt thou behold and see the reward of the wicked.

It is amazing how many Christians cling to the Old Testament and neglect the New, for Christ repeatedly contradicted the idea that God punishes men for their sins by sending them suffering in this life. Yet a well-known modern religious writer has stated that his faith was undermined by the fact that many religious people were killed in the Second World War, contrary to Psalm 91.

11. When our Lord saw a man who was born blind, his disciples asked him, 'Master, who did sin, this man or his parents that he was born blind?' Jesus answered, 'Neither hath this man sinned nor his parents.' (John 9.1–3) In Luke 13.1–5, Christ repeated the same lesson. Men killed by Pilate or by the accidental collapse

of a wall in Siloam were no more sinners than anyone else.

If we think of it, only confusion would result if God always interfered to save the righteous from circumstances. If an air liner crashed, all the passengers would be killed except two earnest Christians who would walk out unscathed. Or, if a party of mountaineers fell over a precipice, all would be killed except one who floats gracefully to the ground unaffected by the force of gravity. God has made the world orderly and dependable, so that we can know how to act.

Nor would the moral results be good. If people knew that sincere Christians were never ill and never met violent deaths, they would regard religion as a practical external benefit, an insurance policy to keep one out of trouble. But true religion is the process of drawing nearer in spirit to God, until we are able to communicate with him and know him directly. It is not a worldly insurance policy.

In Luke 21, our Lord described the many disasters which would afflict the world. In verse 13, the Authorized Version has, 'And it shall turn to you for a testimony'. Later translations seem to make the meaning clearer. J. B. Phillips has, 'This will be your chance to witness for me'. The Jerusalem Bible reads, 'That will be your opportunity to bear witness'. The New English Bible says, 'This will be your opportunity to testify'. Surely this passage provides the key to suffering—it is our opportunity to show the world what the teaching of Christ means to us. We are not just patiently to bear suffering and to resign ourselves to the will of God. We are to turn our misfortunes and our sufferings into something positive for the glory of God.

Paul seems to have grasped this idea in 2 Corinthians 12.7–9, where he tells of his thorn in the flesh—presumably some chronic physical ailment. He tells how he prayed that it might be cured but nothing happened. But then he understood. God said to him that divine strength was made perfect in weakness. So he cries out enthusiastically, 'Most gladly therefore will I rather glory in my infirmities, that the power of Christ may rest upon me'. Our troubles and sufferings are not misfortunes to which we must be resigned, but opportunities to show the world how the indwelling power of God can overcome our handicaps.

E. Stanley Jones in his book, *Christ and Human Suffering*, tells of a little girl baby in China who was dropped by her nurse and her back broken, making her a hopeless cripple for life. At first she was an embittered bad-tempered cripple, constantly complaining. Then one day she became a Christian and suddenly she realized that her crippled state was an opportunity. She became a school teacher, universally loved and admired by successive generations of children.

Another of Stanley Jones' stories tells of a young English girl who was working as a teacher in Rangoon, when she contracted leprosy. She fought back desperately, was taken away for treatment and returned without symptoms. But soon the symptoms reappeared and plunged her into despair. One day she walked out of her classroom and over to the leper asylum a few miles away. She hesitated outside the gates and then with a prayer on her lips she walked in. Suddenly she realized that her disaster was her opportunity. Debarred from her career as a teacher, she became the teacher of the lepers. She also formed them into a choir and taught them to sing. She and her lepers were radiantly happy—a story which helps us to understand Dean Inge's statement, 'Joy as a moral quality is a Christian invention'.

Such stories could be told by the thousand. We do not have to seek them in China or Burma. St Therèse of

Lisieux was born in 1872. At the age of nine she experienced her first serious illness. At sixteen, however, she gained admission to the Carmelite convent of Lisieux. She was constantly ill for the rest of her life and died at the age of twenty-six. I have never seen a medical report on her condition, but it seems probable that she was suffering from consumption, tuberculosis of the lungs, the principal killing disease of the nineteenth century. She suffered intensely from the austerities of the Carmelite rule; for example, she never could get warm in bed at night.

> You are making a great mistake [she wrote in a letter] if you think of me as advancing bravely along the path of self-sacrifice. Every day I learn by experience how weak I am, but our Lord has taught me how to *glory in my infirmities*. One turns away from the sight of one's own wretchedness to look only at Jesus Christ. You ask me what are the means for attaining perfection, but I only know of one: Love. Is there any human being capable of appreciating it, and giving us some return? Only our Lord can do this, and he gives in return infinitely more than we can give him.

In another letter she wrote 'Suffering and persecution bring about the reign of Christ in souls more effectually than eloquent preaching'. To a novice who was pitying herself she said: 'God loves cheerful people who can always manage to smile ... Hide your troubles, and tell our Lord with a song on your lips that you are glad to suffer for his sake.' In a letter to her sister she writes of our Lord, 'He feels having to hurt us, but he knows that it is the only way to teach us how to know him'.

As her end approached she wrote, 'Do not think that I want to leave you, as though it were a greater privilege to die young; I only wish to please our Lord. As he seems to be calling me out of this life, I cannot help rejoicing: for God has no need of anyone, least of all myself, to do good on earth.'

A few night before her death, Sister Geneviève came into the infirmary and found her with eyes raised to heaven and hands joined in prayer.

'What are you doing? You ought to be trying to sleep.'
'I cannot, so I am praying.'
'What do you say to our Lord?'
'Nothing; I was just loving Him.'[1]

Even nearer home is the story of Edith Barfoot told by Sir Basil Blackwell. She was born in 1887 but in 1907, when she was twenty years old, she fell ill and her disease was diagnosed as rheumatoid arthritis. Originally she had planned to devote her life to nursing, but she was destined all her life to be a patient. She lived to the age of eighty-two, having been bedridden for sixty-two years, during most of which time she was in agonizing physical pain. Before her death she became totally blind and deaf.

It is difficult even to imagine a life of such indescribable suffering, yet the strongest impression received by those who visited her was her air of great happiness. In 1928, when she had been crippled and in intense pain for twenty-one years, one of the Cowley Fathers asked her to write a note of her thoughts on suffering. She was then still able to write in bed. She headed her short paper 'The Discovery of Joy in the Vocation of Suffering'. A few extracts must suffice.

> The soul must ever remember that He who calls for her response is God the Father and that always it is the call of Love, no matter how much of hardness and difficulty the call may hold for her. The Great All-Father favours His children by accepting their ready will

[1] These extracts are taken from *Just for Today* compiled by a Benedictine of Stanbrook Abbey, with a foreword by Monsignor Ronald Knox.

in Love's own way and this is the way of sacrifice which spells suffering in the most acute form: for love in this world always involves suffering.

The Father asks His child to give up all, and she is probably dismayed as she realizes what this giving up is going to mean; for she had in past days unwillingly tried to bargain, . . . making surrender of only part of her will to Him but keeping back part of it . . . or as she would have explained in those days, to use for Him in the way that was her own, but which she hoped might be His way.

Because it is simply the call to follow Him in this particular vocation of pain-bearing and helplessness, the soul senses the joy which the call holds for her . . . She must give a willing response, whole-hearted, complete, thorough. She must not keep anything back nor be rebellious at anything . . .

The soul's response must be an active, alert response to the Father's call . . . Thus in the vocation of suffering God shows the soul many spiritual opportunities for helping in His great work of love.

How great a comfort it can be to us to know that there is nothing in this life which we need to fear. For God's strength will always be sufficient for us, a strength which is made perfect in our weakness if he really dwells in our souls. Suffering, then, can be an opportunity for us to advance more rapidly towards communion with God. In the words of Teilhard de Chardin, an overplus of Spirit can be born from a deficiency of nature.

Von Hügel writes in his peculiar quiet manner that we should persevere in our gentle attempts gently to will whatever suffering God may kindly send us. He speaks of 'the grand practice of at once meeting suffering with joy. God alone can help us to succeed in this: but what is Christianity if it be not something like that.'

19 *Liaison*

I remember once seeing an interview between a reporter and an archbishop. The reporter asked, 'Have you *ever* asked God in prayer for something and subsequently received it?' He spoke with the cocky half-amused contempt with which an adult might address a child, 'Did you see Father Christmas come down the chimney, dear?' His words not only seemed to proclaim that he thought that he was talking down to someone of inferior intellect, but also that he believed that prayer consisted in asking God for things.

It may, therefore, be worthwhile to begin this chapter by contradicting the idea that Christians regard God as a kind of sugar-daddy who can be persuaded to give them nice presents if they ask him politely. The gifts desired are probably entirely limited to this world—a kind of shopping list of things which we should like to have.

The shopping list conception of prayer soon involves us in a number of questions which are obviously absurd. Firstly, if God knows everything, why do we have to tell him about our troubles? Yet some people seem to think it necessary to explain their circumstances to God in order to persuade him of their need.

If God is so loving, we may be asked, why does he not rescue us without our praying him to do so?

If God knows what is going to happen in the future, what is the use of asking him to change it?

If God has decided to do a certain thing, will our prayers persuade him to change his mind?

Is God so forgetful that he will not remember us unless we remind him that we are here?

Clever people can display their wit by asking such questions in order to show their contempt for such 'myths'. This enables them to feel gratifyingly superior until troubles come, and they find themselves alone and in despair in face of a cold hostile world.

All these questions are the result of thinking of God as if he were another man. We cannot imagine an infinite Spirit who not only fills the Universe but our own souls also, just as the air envelops the whole earth and also fills our lungs. We do not know how our prayers are received by him, for he is already within us, helping us to pray to himself.

A further and more reasonable objection to making our prayers petitions for worldly benefits is that we do not really know what to ask. Is it reasonable for me to pray that my son will come out top of his class at school? Other fathers may be praying that their sons will be top also? Would it not be better to allow the best pupil to win? But I could well pray God to guide my son through the Spirit working in his soul. Am I justified in asking God to prevent my losing my employment which enables me to support my family? For all I know, if I were dismissed, I might be led into a better and more productive career. Such things have happened to me.

Most of us can remember stages in our lives when we were passionately desirous of obtaining a certain appointment or of moving to another country, but failed to realize our hopes. As it turned out later, however, it was very fortunate that we did not achieve these ambitions for in fact we eventually found a far more fruitful activity. If our early prayers had been granted, we should never have won any success or rendered any useful service. In brief, the difficulty about praying for our worldly desires is that we do not know what is best for us.

Enough has been said to show that we all need to say to God what the apostles said to Christ, 'Lord teach us to pray,' for we have no idea how we should even begin. Prayer is a supernatural activity which we must ask God to produce in us. In the words of Jean-Nicolas Grou, in his little book, *How to Pray*: 'Prayer is in itself a wholly spiritual act, addressed to Him who is the supreme Spirit, the Spirit who sees all things and is present in all things and is, as St Augustine says, more closely united to our soul than its deepest depths.'

If we love anyone, we enjoy speaking to them. If we love God, we shall want to be always speaking to him. So the first prayer we may use is one asking God to help us to love him. As we begin to love him, we shall begin to pray. In fact, as we shall see again later, it may not be necessary even to use words. To think of God with love is to pray. But there is no need for us to speculate on how we should pray, for Christ, as everyone knows, has left us a model prayer. The Lord's Prayer consists of seven sentences. The first three sentences are devoted to praising God and asking for the extension of his kingdom. The fourth asks him to give us the necessities of life. The fifth begs him to forgive us our failures and our crimes. The sixth and the seventh beseech him to help us to do better in the future.

We see that the prayer commences with adoration and praise. The words 'Our Father' emphasize a loving relationship. By saying 'Our' in place of 'My', we associate ourselves with the whole human race which, sharing the same Father, consists of our brothers and sisters. We try and achieve some dim inkling of the eternity, immensity, omniscience and omnipotence of the vast Spirit which created the universe, as compared with our own tininess, weakness, cowardice, worldliness and insignificance. And yet we believe that he knows and loves each one of us. It is not that God is in need of praise from such tiny insects as us. But when we realize his vast power and glory and the fact that he knows each one of us, we cannot restrain our joy and our gratitude.

Our minds are so limited to thinking in terms of human affairs that we feel that no one could possibly know and love everyone. Some people cannot believe in a God who has a personal relationship with each one of us, because they visualize him as a big man. Thus the first part of our prayer must consist not only of wonder and joy at the splendour and greatness of God but also of humility—some attempt to realize our own nothingness. As Evelyn Underhill writes in *The Golden Sequence*:

> The more deeply we enter the worshipping life, the more profoundly we experience the otherness of that which we adore, and the more deeply purifying is the failure of our understanding before the reality of God . . . One side of our response to Spirit must always be a humble acknowledgement of our ignorance . . . [For God] has a certain kinship with the creature, which He is ever moulding from within and without. Spirit indwells and penetrates the soul's very fabric as a quiet love; and it is here in our ground that we are to experience the most intimate and transforming realities of prayer. . . .
>
> The life of prayer in its full and balanced development unites a width and depth of vision with a great interior dependence and intimacy.

The first three sentences of the Lord's Prayer are thus occupied with adoration, praise and thanksgiving to God and with hopes of the establishment of his kingdom on earth. The fourth sentence, 'Give us this day our daily bread,' acknowledges our complete dependence on him and asks him to give us whatever is necessary. The fifth, sixth and seventh sentences also concern ourselves and our spiritual needs. We ask to be forgiven our shortcomings, on condition that we forgive those who offend against us.

The last two sentences ask God's help to enable us to serve him better.

We see then that the sample prayer left by our Lord conveys no suggestion whatever that prayer is a means of obtaining worldly favours or benefits from God. It suggests rather a conversation, an exchange of communications with him, in which we admit our dependence, praise him for his glory, and ask him to continue his help to us in our spiritual lives.

When instructing his disciples how to pray, our Lord told them to enter their private apartment, close the door and pray to their Father who is in secret. Our private prayers will doubtless be on the lines of his model prayer, and will begin by an attempt to realize his splendour and our nothingness. These thoughts result in praise, thanksgiving, and prayers for the extension of his influence.

The second part of our private prayers may be something for ourselves. In John 14.14–15, our Lord said: 'If ye shall ask anything in my name, I will do it. If ye love me keep my commandments.' We may, I think, assume that the phrase 'in my name' means according to his commandments, or according to his system. It would be absurd to claim that he meant that if we asked for a million pounds in the bank, it would immediately be credited to our account. Thus I think that the second part of our prayer should really be to ask for help to advance in the spiritual life.

We speak to God because we love him. Consequently I do not see why we should not also confide our worldly troubles to him, as we would consult any dear friend. I do think, however, that we should avoid giving God detailed orders on how he should help us. We confide our worries to him, which eases our own anxiety, but we leave it to him to rescue us as he sees best.

God desires to draw all men to himself, but it is his policy to do so by love and not by compulsion. God is an immense Spirit filling the universe, while men are tiny insects, fighting, struggling and working in the world. How is God to arrest the attention of men and explain himself to them? The answer seems to be—through other men.

Christ was the supreme example of a man who, by his way of life, showed the nature of God to men. This process is known as incarnation—the Divine Spirit inhabiting a man. I hope that I am not being blasphemous when I suggest that the process of incarnation is still used, though on an immeasurably lower scale. The efforts of Christian people to raise their own spiritual status have sometimes been denounced as a selfish attempt to win their own salvation in cynical indifference to the rest of mankind. But God's method of drawing men to himself seems to be principally by the use of his Holy Spirit in the souls of men and women. If this be true, it is not wrong or selfish to try and draw the Holy Spirit into our souls. On the contrary it is the only way by which we can serve God.

Christ did not classify and record the intellectual arguments which prove the existence of God. Yet no one can dispute that he changed the history of the human race. This he did by just living as a man among men. It was the influence of his personality radiating on all around him, which changed the world.

All down history we see the same effect produced by holiness. One saint, by the quality of his life, can bring thousands of persons to God. Those who pray God to cleanse and strengthen their own lives cannot therefore be accused of selfishness. Their object is not to 'save' their own souls, but to become useful instruments in the service of God. As far as we can see, the highest rôle which a human being can play is to be a pipeline—a transmitter of God's love to others.

We have to pass on his love untarnished, not our own kindness, good nature or courtesy. To become such a transmitter is a task which we shall not completely accomplish in a lifetime, and of which without his help we shall achieve nothing at all. To beg him to enable us to serve him in this manner will, therefore, constitute the second part of our prayer.

It is only when we come to the third part of our prayer that we begin to ask for specified things. A few such requests may be for help to ourselves. For example we might ask his help in a speech we have to make, or on a journey which we are obliged to undertake. Principally, however, we shall ask for his help to people or causes. It is difficult to pray for people in great detail, because we do not know what is best for them. So we shall probably limit ourselves to asking him to bless and to guide them and to draw them into nearer communion with himself. We may ask his aid also for persons in positions of responsibility, the Queen, the President, the Prime Minister and other public servants. Similarly we may ask him to guide and bless the clergy and our own parish priests.

Finally let us remember that prayer must be a two-way communication. We confide our thoughts to him, but we must also wait quietly and listen for his answers. This is often more difficult than it is to speak to him. We are interested in what we are trying to say to him, but when we have finished our minds become filled with all the worldly duties we should be performing. It is difficult to sit quietly and listen. Yet I have been impressed by the immense numbers of people all through history who have believed that God has guided them. To take one example at random, Abraham Lincoln is reported to have said: 'I am satisfied that when the Almighty wants me to do or not to do any particular thing, He finds a way of letting me know it.'

Perhaps we could best describe our private prayers as liaison. They are not requests for worldly benefits, but an attempt to keep in touch with our Headquarters, to enable us to render better service.

✠

Before leaving the subject, I would like to refer to family prayers. When I was a boy, we had family prayers every morning after breakfast. My father would read one or two prayers, usually including that 'for all sorts and conditions of men', and the General Thanksgiving from the Anglican Prayer Book, which I have remembered by heart ever since. Everybody came into the room for prayers, including the cook and the housemaid if we had such, or other domestic helpers.

This was perhaps rather an established routine, but at least it reminded us of God before the day's work began. After leaving school, I remained unmarried for twenty-four years without a family, mostly in distant lands without even having a home. Unfortunately, when I did marry, I did not return to my father's custom of family prayers, which I now believe, looking back, to have had so profound an effect on my young life. In my own family, however, we have always said grace before meals, an opportunity at least to remember God three times a day.

20 *Conversation Piece*

In Luke 18.1, our Lord is reported as saying that men ought always to pray and not to faint or be discouraged. In the fifth chapter of his first letter to the Thessalonians, St Paul wrote: 'Rejoice ever more, pray without ceasing. In everything give thanks.' If we visualize prayer only as retiring into our closet, shutting the door and praying to our Father in secret, then obviously we cannot do it always or without ceasing. We all have our work to do, whether in an office, driving a vehicle, organizing a business or doing manual work in a factory or on a farm. How can we pray without ceasing if our minds are fully occupied with our daily work? The command to pray always and without ceasing has exercised the minds of many religious writers.

The Orthodox Church has sometimes tried to carry it out by the use of the Jesus prayer. This consists in repeating continuously the short sentence, 'Lord Jesus Christ, have mercy upon me'. Many are said to have attained sanctity by this means. To others it seems exposed to the danger of becoming mere unthinking repetition.

Many people have attempted to devise systems to recall their minds to God throughout the day. One man I knew offered up a quick prayer whenever he heard the clock strike. Possibly the medieval hair-shirt was intended not only to inflict irritation on the wearer, but also to recall his mind to God, whenever he felt a desire to scratch! Ministers of religion are perhaps too much inclined to urge us to come to church on Sundays, without laying sufficient emphasis on our trying to keep in God's presence all through the week.

A short shaft of prayer pierces heaven, says the medieval author of *The Cloud of Unknowing*, using the simile of an arrow. We may call out from the midst of our work or our recreation, 'O God, I love Thee', 'Lord Jesus, have mercy on me', 'O Lord help me to love you more'. For a moment we think lovingly of our Father and then turn back to our work.

A well-known little book on this subject is *The Practice of the Presence of God* by Brother Lawrence, a lay brother in a Carmelite community in Paris, who died in 1691. We should, he said, establish in ourselves a sense of God's presence by continually conversing with him; it was a shameful thing, he thought, to quit his conversation to think of trifles and fooleries. Having resolved to make the love of God the end of all his actions, he was well-satisfied with his method. He was pleased when he could take up a straw from the ground for the love of God.

Saint Therèse of Lisieux wrote, 'It seems to me that prayer is just the raising of one's heart and an upward glance to heaven, a cry of love and gratitude in the midst of trials as much as in joy. It is being lifted on to a higher supernatural plane, where the soul is enlarged and united to God.'

The secret of unceasing prayer is love of God. If we love another human being devotedly, the thought of him or her is constantly at the back of our minds. We feel happy at our work in the office, on the road or in the kitchen because the thought of our love is always with us, though it does not prevent our writing a report or cooking the dinner. Sometimes our love is in the unconscious, sometimes it emerges to consciousness.

In the same way, if we truly love God we shall always want to be thinking of him and talking to him. But how are we to love him like that? Here we must return to the mystery of the spiritual life. Our physical bodies are geared to the material world around us. It is the Spirit dwelling in our souls which enables us to appreciate the spiritual world. God within us enables us to communicate with God in the universe. The first step, therefore, is to abandon ourselves entirely to God and to beg him to come and live in our souls.

When he does so, he will assist us continually to remember him, if we do not obstruct him. Thus an effort on our part is necessary if we are to be constantly in contact. This does not mean that our surface mind must always be occupied with God, but that love of him will always be in the depth of our minds, ready to rise at frequent intervals to consciousness.

To live in this atmosphere of prayer is not a hindrance to our efficiency in carrying out our duties but the reverse. To begin with, our work becomes easier and lighter if we offer it to him. This does not mean actual religious duties, but the normal occupations of the day, writing, digging, hammering, cooking, driving—these actions are necessary to support the community and can all be done for the love of God. Doing everything for God makes us more cheerful at our work and more energetic. Moreover it makes it easier for us to bear responsibility, for all we are doing is for him and he will guide us and provide the strength we need.

Our happiness and our freedom from strain will make us more sociable, more genial and more obliging with our colleagues at work, and with all the people whom we meet in the world. It enables us to be cheerful, carefree and amusing, to speak tactfully and with good nature, and to listen sympathetically to people who wish to tell us their views or their problems.

We can live in this atmosphere of constant prayer, although our surface minds are free to devote themselves to every task which confronts them. No one knows that we are always praying and no one is embarrassed or inconvenienced by it. Indeed if we learned really to pray without ceasing, we should be pleasant company to all who meet us, because the love of God, not our own social gifts, would shine through all that we say and do.

We are indeed faced by only two alternatives. We may reject all idea of religion and the spiritual life. Or we must dedicate ourselves to the service of God and our neighbour. Half measures will always be ineffective. If we go to church on Sunday and pray at home in the morning and the evening, we shall have to go through seven or eight hours every day engrossed in our daily work. So long a period of immersion in worldly affairs will cause us to dry up and become nervy, irritable and frightened. The only cure for this condition is a fresh intake of spiritual strength. If we could remain continuously in contact with God, our courage, humility and good humour would never run low. We should remain, as it were, always plugged in to the mains, instead of relying on re-charging our batteries in the morning and the evening alone.

It is, therefore, not only possible but essential for us to keep constantly in touch with God all the day long. To some extent this can be done by the use of continual short prayers or aspirations. 'O God help me', 'O God, teach me how to love Thee more', 'O God my Father, I belong solely to Thee'. 'O Lord Jesus, I implore Thee to fill my whole soul with Thy Spirit'. 'O Lord I beseech Thee at all times to direct and rule my heart'. Sometimes these calls for help can be more specific. 'Dear Father, show me what to say to this man.' 'O Lord, help me to speak calmly and affectionately to this angry customer.' 'O Lord support me with your power through this long day's physical strain.'

The truth is, however, that we tend to use words because we do so when communicating with other people, but it is not essential to do so when speaking to God. He is always there and knows our needs without our asking.

We pray chiefly to remind ourselves of his constant presence. As a result, we can often dispense with words. Just to turn our thoughts silently to him in loyalty and affection will often be enough.

To pray without ceasing is to maintain constant contact with God, to whose service we are ready to devote our lives. It is to remain at all times immersed in the atmosphere of his Spirit, saturated with his viewpoint, so that we reflect his loving compassion for all mankind. Trying to live as St Paul intended when he said, 'We have the mind of Christ'.

✠

Is it not also possible that the practice of praying without ceasing may ultimately break down the denominational barriers which still superficially separate Christians from one another, but which no longer represent any real differences between us? To pray in our souls without ceasing is to practise a pure spiritual activity which is the same in all denominations, in all countries and in all ages. It would give us a religion of direct contact with God's Spirit, unobstructed by man-made formulas, or by misguided loyalty to our own little sect. For are not our subdivisions due, like so much else, to the narrowness and smallness of our minds?

The atmosphere of unceasing communion with God will not make an imposing show at religious conferences or in the press, for it has no worldly hierarchy and no organization or propaganda. It has passed beyond these mundane considerations to unite us in one worldwide family of God's children, an immense army of brothers and sisters, united by their silent and unseen dedication to the Creator Spirit of the universe, who is yet closer to us than breathing and nearer than hands and feet.

In this violent world, so full of hatred and greed, in

which the worldly derive so much satisfaction at the alleged emptiness of our churches, this great rising tide of unceasing prayers may one day silently flood the world, filling it with the spiritual knowledge of God as the waters cover the sea.

It is encouraging to think that God created and maintains the world. It is absurd to think that any human activity can defeat the Creator. Good people who fear that the knowledge and love of God may soon disappear from the world are unnecessarily disturbed. But it may be that, at this particular moment in time, formal worship in churches in our country is less general than it was. If this is the case, it may be more than balanced by the ever increasing spiritual activity of persons unceasingly seeking God in the depth of their souls.

21 *Community Worship*

In Matthew 18.20, we read that our Lord said, 'Where two or three are gathered together in my name, there am I in the midst of them'. Indeed when we remember our twofold duty to love God and our neighbour, it seems only natural that we should gather together with our brothers and sisters to worship God together. To do so not only enables us to worship, praise and speak to our Father but it draws us nearer in love and sympathy to our fellow Christians.

Nevertheless we must appreciate that the object of worship is to acknowledge the existence of a supreme Ruler of the world, the pervading Spirit who directs all life, who is entirely distinct from ourselves and who, to our human minds, is an impenetrable mystery. God alone matters, and God alone is self-existent, distinct from us though not separate or aloof. 'Wherein does your prayer consist,' said St John of the Cross to one of his penitents. To which she answered, 'In considering the beauty of God and in rejoicing that he has such beauty'. This pure and ecstatic joy in the splendour of our Lord and Creator is well expressed in the hymn of the seraphs—'Holy, Holy, Holy, Lord God of hosts, heaven and earth are full of Thy glory'.

When we appreciate that the first object of public worship is to glorify and rejoice in the splendour of our Creator and Father, it seems to be tragic in the extreme that the manner of offering our public worship has so often given rise to bitter controversy. For the second object of public worship is to help us to constitute a loving community of brothers and sisters in his service.

Certain forms of prayer, symbols and ritual are closely associated with treasured memories of our childhood and youth, and changes in the familiar words and ceremonies cause us emotional distress. On this question, man, half-animal and half-spirit, is faced with a constant dilemma. His animal side makes it impossible for him to live solely in a spiritual world. He must needs have something material to hold on to, if he is to visualize spiritual truths and absorb them. His longings and his conceptions do not become actual to him unless they are expressed in words, actions and symbols. But it is precisely here that we encounter our principal danger. It is so easy for the symbol or the ritual to take the place of the spiritual prayer, the outward and visible sign to replace the inward and spiritual grace. Yet the very process of doing things together, bowing, kneeling, reciting or singing do facilitate the unity of the congregation. The whole history of public worship tends to oscillate back and forth in accordance with the twofold nature of man, the material and the spiritual.

We cross ourselves or use crucifixes as material symbols to remind us of the crucifixion of Christ. But then the crucifix or the icon itself becomes an object of worship, or the exact performance of the ritual acts and the correct repetition of the sacred phrases come to be regarded as the essential duties of religion. Then follows the spiritual reaction. A portion of the congregation breaks away, rejects all formal prayers, all written liturgies, all symbols and ceremonies. Soon a rival denomination is set up, worshipping in any available building, with no written prayers or sacred ornaments. Yet both parties are deeply sincere.

If only we could realize that men are half-spirit and half-animal, balancing precariously on a tightrope. Inevitably they sometimes lean to one side and sometimes to the other. There is no sovereign cure for this dilemma, for we are created thus. But likewise there is no possible excuse for cutting ourselves off from one another, or supporting rival organizations. Let us trim the boat as she rocks from side to side, but let us fully and sincerely appreciate that we are all in the same boat.

The use of more or of fewer symbols and ceremonies is a matter of compromise or adjustment but certainly not of hostility. I often think of poor John Bunyan, who spent many years in prison because he would not accept a written prayer book. He had a little daughter born blind of whom he was passionately fond. When he was arrested and taken to prison, saying goodbye to her, he records, was like tearing the flesh from his bones. Yet we can see that there is something to be said both for written and for impromptu prayers.

✠

The simple anthropomorphic minds of medieval artists, who pictured the devil in human form with horns and a tail, have resulted in modern times in disbelief in his existence, but it is difficult to avoid the impression that definite forces of evil do exist. Moreover one of their commonest tricks is to approach us disguised in sheep's clothing, that is, to make use of our most generous emotions in order to sow hatred and discord. They do not attempt to act upon us by exhorting us to do evil, but by admonishing us to do good. 'Be loyal to your congregation,' they urge us, 'you cannot betray your own church and your brothers and sisters in Christ.' They remind us of our duty to stand firm against the heresies of the church down the road.

Our minds are so small that we cannot see through these obvious confidence tricks. Inflated with our own heroism, we sternly declare that we shall never compromise with our fellow Christians who employ a procedure differing slightly from our own. How utterly absurd our petty disputes appear, when we try to visualize them in the setting of the creation of the universe and of the universal Spirit, so vast and so benevolent towards the whole world. Is it right for the minister to wear a dark suit or a white surplice? Does your priest cross himself or wear coloured vestments? We will never surrender an inch to such practices! What poor petty little creatures we are! Surely it is time for us to throw away these prejudices. We should be prepared to pray in any Christian place of worship, and all churches should give a loving welcome to Christians of any denomination, though we may readily admit that it is easier to pray in one's own church, where one is at home, because the words and the procedures are familiar.

No two human beings in the world are identical—a staggering thought when we consider the millions of human beings alive. As God made us all different, it seems to be obvious that he does not want us all to be the same. Apart, therefore, from the prejudices which we inherit from our sectarian background, we should recognize that various forms of service make a greater or less appeal to different people. An example is to be found in music. Some people are profoundly musical, and find delight and inspiration in the most beautiful music which they can produce. To others the music is an obstacle to worship. We are in church to worship and to communicate with God. When we speak to the people whom we know and love, we do not sing to them—we talk to them. In the same way I want in church to speak to God. When the Lord's Prayer is chanted by the choir, I do not feel that I am praying. Other people derive inspiration from prayers which are sung. This seems to be merely a question of our individual constitutions.

Some people in the same way like highly decorated churches with sacred pictures hung on the walls and stained-glass windows. Others worship God in what seems little more than a whitewashed shed. These also are doubtless differences of temperament. Yet even such personal differences lead to schisms. A great leader may think that ornamented churches are a vanity which divert our attention from the shining purity of God. He sets up a sect of his own, who worship in a whitewashed barn. But later generations of his congregation may be profoundly artistic and musical. A more artistic service would appeal to them more deeply. But meanwhile the plain whitewashed chapel has become a matter of conscience. *Never* would they consent to darken the doors of *that place* down the road where they actually use incense. O dear! O dear! How very small we are!

So much for our petty narrow sectarianisms when compared to the splendour and the glory of God. It is the fashion nowadays to complain that church is so dull. Some clergy endeavour to render it more interesting by introducing modern music, young people's orchestras, mimes or other diversions. We lose sight of the fact that the centre of every religious service is God. As we may go to a reception at Buckingham Palace or the White House to meet the head of the state, so we go to church to meet the head of the universe.

When we enter, we kneel to make our obeisance to him. In every prayer and in every hymn, we are speaking to our King. The fact that we are surrounded by our brothers and sisters makes the whole process more inspiring, but the basis of the entire procedure is that it is addressed to God who is presiding at the meeting. We may begin by confessing our shortcomings, our insignificance and our carelessness. We continue by praising him for his greatness, his mercy and his patience. We listen to his word in the Bible, or partake of the bread and wine which Christ established in remembrance of his passion. In all these activities, we must ourselves take an active part, addressing ourselves to God in all the prayers and hymns, and ourselves personally confessing our private sins and offering our personal thanks. If we think of what we are saying and truly address ourselves to God, we shall not find the service dull.

It is also, I think, important to realize that a lively and engrossing church service depends on the quality of our lives during the week. If all the week we have been totally engrossed in our own business or pleasure, these subjects will still fill our thoughts during the hour we spend at church. We shall only dimly hear the parson droning away, while we re-live that interview with the manager on Friday, or mentally draft the letter we want to write to the bank when we get home. But if we believe that God is able to communicate with us, our attention will be held by our desire to speak to him, and by our earnest hope that he will come and dwell in our souls and give us guidance and peace.

The true object of our conversation with God, therefore, is to bring our thinking into line with his will. Can we place ourselves so far in sympathy with his will that we shall become satellites, receiving his wishes and reflecting them back to the world about us?

There has recently been a tendency on television to replace church services by discussion between intellectuals and philosophers on moral subjects. These changes seem to indicate a complete failure to understand the nature of a church service, which appears to be looked upon as a minister of religion talking to his congregation. A conversation between clever intellectuals may well be more entertaining than a sermon addressed by a parson to his flock. But a religious service does not consist of a minister of religion talking to people. It is the minister leading his congregation in speaking to God.

Moreover Christianity is not a system of morals deduced from the logical and reasoned discussions of philosophers. It is a way of life revealed to us by our Father and Creator. He is ready to grant us this revelation if we ask for it sincerely and open our souls to him for its reception. In this event, he will himself enter our souls and act as our guide and our strength through life.

A religious service is thus a gathering of clergy and people who together address themselves to God, who presides over the meeting. Together they praise and thank God for his glory, beg his forgiveness for their past failures and implore him to accept them and to fill their souls with his Spirit to enable them to lead a life of devoted service to him and to their neighbours. Without the indwelling of his Spirit we cannot achieve such a life. If we cannot join our brothers and sisters in church in speaking to God, we may yet do so in spirit by watching a service on television, but not by listening to a discussion by philosophers.

We all know that we ought to lead a moral life, but the point is that in practice we never succeed in doing so. It is only with the help of the indwelling Spirit of God that we are *able* to lead good lives. The object of a religious service is to ask God to give us his Spirit to enable us to serve him and our neighbours.

One last subject may be worth including at this point. It is that prayer involves also an obligation. It is easy in church to say amen to a prayer for the poor and the starving, and then to go home to a large Sunday dinner. If we ask God to feed the hungry, we surely incur the obligation to do what we can to help them ourselves. In this connection, it often seems to me curious how many modern prayers are in the imperative. 'Heal the sick, cheer the lonely, feed the hungry, comfort the bereaved'. Having thus issued our curt orders to our Creator, we walk home feeling the self-satisfaction of having done our duty. Of course this idea does not enter the minds of those who use these prayers, but I cannot quite avoid the suspicion that, although unconsciously, our modern arrogance does partly inspire those who compose such prayers. We *do* think we know what ought to be done.

22 *Love*

A year ago I was obliged to go into hospital for a surgical operation. When I arrived in the ward, I unpacked my bag, undressed, got into bed and lay reading a book. A nurse came up to see if I was comfortable, and asked me what I was reading. I held up the book for her to see. It was Thomas Merton's *The Power and Meaning of Love*. 'You naughty old man,' she sniggered, 'I'll tell your wife when she comes to see you.' Thomas Merton was a monk of the Cistercian Order of the Strict Observance. The love of which he wrote was the love of God. Perhaps it is typical of the age in which we live that the word love has fallen from its high estate to be something common and vulgar, over which young people can giggle.

God is love, we are told—a beautiful phrase to which we do not devote much thought. Let us pause for a moment and try to consider what it means. We believe that the world, and indeed the universe, was created by an inconceivably vast, splendid, eternal, infinite and omniscient Power. The Creator was and is of a completely different order from our tiny selves. He is Spirit, a word we use for want of a better, owing to the utter inadequacy of human language. Spirit is invisible to human eyes, yet it permeates creation and supports and envelops our ephemeral lives. When, therefore, we say that God is love, we mean that the whole driving force and controlling power of the universe is saturated with goodwill towards its creatures. It is possible to argue that the world we see around us does not appear to be directed by love. But it is *not* possible to deny that the most important question in our lives is whether it is so or not. 'God is love' is not a pretty, pious phrase, but the key to the comprehension of life.

The Book of Genesis tells us that man was created to have dominion over all the earth—to be, as it were, the agent of God in governing the world. The language of the story of the creation seems to us quaint, but it appears to conceal a remarkable amount of wisdom and knowledge. If we recognize that man was intended to be God's agent on earth, and if we have grasped the significance of the phrase, 'God is Love', then it is obvious that man ought himself to have followed the principle of his Master's policy, that is to say, that he should have looked upon all creation with love.

It is obvious that if God feels affection for the whole of his creation, but that his agent in charge chooses to abandon and contradict his Master's policy, then the whole world will be thrown into chaos, which in fact is its condition today. Some of course will here say impatiently that these are all silly old fables ('myths' is the modern word) and that man is merely an animal, produced by the survival of the fittest. But we have already seen that this theory does not explain anything. For materialism is only negative. It cannot produce an alternative to spirit. It can only criticize men's efforts to find the Spirit, but itself has no explanation to offer. For man is *not* just an animal struggling to survive. He has a soul as well as a body. All through history, as we can trace it, man's battles to survive have been interspersed with movements of love, toleration, self-sacrifice, martyrdom, or in other words by the stirrings of Love, which by definition is God. Thus we find man to be a contradiction, a continual battlefield, torn by an endless struggle between good and evil.

It is no use our speculating how this situation originated. We are obliged always to keep reminding ourselves of our own smallness. What sort of a God would our Father be if *we* could understand him? We are so easily carried away by the exuberance of our own cleverness, that I personally at least find it absolutely vital frequently to stop and ask myself, 'Who do you think you are, little man?' I do not know how evil came into the world, and I realize that I cannot and am not intended to know the explanation.

I can dimly apprehend that our own training makes it necessary for us to bear spiritual, mental and physical suffering in this life. Looking at the people around me, I can often observe that those whom I most admire are those who have come through great tribulation. Thus, whatever the origins of evil may be, I can realize that God uses the sufferings inflicted upon us by evil to mould us according to his wishes. It is of vital importance to keep our minds always facing in this direction. God is love, we are his agents on earth, therefore we also must be love, if we are loyally to carry out our Master's policy.

We are so utterly obsessed and so completely pre-occupied with our daily lives on earth that we continually and perhaps unexpectedly find ourselves facing in the wrong direction. Instead of devoting ourselves as his agents to furthering God's will on earth, we find ourselves trying to use him to further *our* worldly interests. An article recently appeared in a British publication with the heading, 'How Jesus can be fitted into our ideas'. The article was serious and well meant, but I could not help feeling staggered at the mentality which could produce such a title. Can the boundless universe and its Creator be 'fitted into' my back garden?

I cannot avoid returning again and again to this question of our basic outlook. Are we humble servants, trying to serve God in the extension of his policy on earth? Or are we solely dedicated to our earthly ambitions and preoccupations, and do we try and make God fit into our ideas? Do we hope for a religious revival because it would be useful to us? It might reduce our crime statistics and the expenses incurred by the state in providing for illegitimate children or juvenile delinquents. Why should not God be useful to men?

Love then is not a sentimental theme, and still less is it the mutual attraction of the sexes. It is the key to the motivation of the universe. If we try to tune in, as it were, to the wave-length on which God looks at the universe, we shall be co-operating with our Master's plan, even if only on the diminutive scale on which we exist. We shall regard the whole world with equal benevolence, for he sends his rain alike on the just and on the unjust.

There are many people in Britain who give themselves devotedly to public service, or to private charities. For all of them the parable of the sheep and the goats holds out hopes (Matthew 25.31–46). For when the King says to those on his right hand that they are blessed of the Father, because they gave food to him when he was hungry and clothing to him when he was naked, they are surprised. 'When saw we thee hungry, thirsty, naked and a stranger, and fed thee, clothed thee and took thee in?' they ask. And the King replies, 'Inasmuch as ye have done it unto one of the least of these my brethren, ye have done it unto me'. They had not loved and helped other people for specifically 'religious' reasons, but just out of love. But God is love. We may reject 'religion' because of intellectual doubts or human rivalries, but if there is love in our hearts, God is there though we do not realize his presence.

In former times, each small town or institution, or even private houses in the country, used to have their own power station or electric generating plants, for their private use. Now all the power stations in the country are linked into one great network, which supplies electricity to the whole nation on a single plan. In the same way, God's love supports, guides and blesses all mankind, but we like to have our own little charities, each according to our own ideas, independent of the mainstream of God's power and benevolence. Are we not sometimes flattering our own little vanities, and perhaps secretly admiring our own goodness?

Would it not be better for us to take a wider view, and each one of us to contribute his tiny effort to help the divine overall plan? Let us forget the national and sectarian differences with which our little minds are so preoccupied, and each pour his or her tiny trickle of love into the swelling tide of God's benevolence towards mankind.

We see thus that love is an attitude of good will to all creation. It is our vocation to be God's children and to help on the family business, which means that we must learn to love as God loves. This willed love is not a sentiment but a dynamic power. Its object is to win the whole world from its present chaos and anarchy and bring it into harmony with God.

To achieve this end, the human race must be led out of the jungle of its own hates, fears and greeds into the open, sunlit plains of God's peace and love and mutual co-operation. It is not our duty to save our own souls by giving our time to prayer, worship and reading. Our task is to help the establishment of God's spiritual dominion of unity and peace all over the world.

Yet it is true at the same time that our first duty is to make ourselves as perfect as we can—not with the selfish object of winning salvation for ourselves, but because only dedicated lives are useful in God's service. We often forget that we are not asked to give our money or our time only, but to give *ourselves*. He who loses his life in this sense, gains everything. In 1 Corinthians 13.3, Paul says, 'Though I bestow all my goods to feed the poor, and though I give my body to be burned, and have not love, it profits me nothing'. We may conscientiously give a tenth of our possessions to charity or to the church, but the result will not accomplish much unless we give ourselves.

If, however, we give the whole of our lives, the results will be incalculable, for influence is one of the most powerful forces in the world, though it cannot be totted up on a balance sheet. It has the advantage of being impossible to assess. We may be proud of our financial contributions to charity, but we cannot be proud if we exert a beneficial influence on others, because we shall probably not be aware of it. Indeed, if our influence is to be of any value, it cannot originate from ourselves. We cannot, and we are not expected to, possess any useful influence which we can pass on to the world. Our sole duty is to be a pipeline—so to open ourselves to God's Spirit, that it will overflow from us and reach other people. One saint thus filled with God, may, unknown to himself, turn tens of thousands of persons to love God, his influence sometimes extending for centuries after his own death.

Missionaries in far countries do not convert people by teaching them to read and write, or even to believe religious dogma, but by their example in the giving of themselves. A life completely abandoned to God's will and to God's love, will draw all those who see it to God.

Some of the wise spiritual writers of former times used to advise their readers to overcome a vice, not by fighting it, but by actively cultivating the opposite virtue. It does not require any great perspicacity on our part to realize that the world has been thrown into chaos by the rivalries, jealousies and hatreds of men. Indeed it is no exaggeration to say that, without God's mercy, the extermination of the human race is threatened by these intense hates. Let us not be satisfied to paper over the cracks by suggesting compromises in these bitter enmities. Let us throw ourselves body and soul into the opposite camp. Let us selflessly pour out all the love of which God makes us capable on the whole human race, utterly forgetful of any personal considerations.

Our first task then—our first contribution to the spiritual conquest of the world—is to give ourselves to God and to our neighbours, keeping nothing back.

✠

Love, first of all therefore, is an act of the will, a decision to give ourselves and our whole lives to service. For this purpose, a moving spiritual conversion is not enough. In times of coldness, doubt, sickness or trouble, resolute action of the will is required.

But though we like to think of ourselves as guided by our reason, in practice human emotions are much more powerful than rationality. It is not enough to serve God and our neighbour coldly by a sheer act of will power. Our love must be not only a dynamic driving force but a warm emotion. We learn to love God by thinking about him, by continually talking to him all the day long, and by constantly remembering his presence inside us and all around us.

We learn to love by actually serving and loving other people, and our love kindles their emotions of love, so that our warm affections continue to expand. 'Where you do not find love, put in your love, and then you will find love,' wrote St John of the Cross. Love is the only source of human happiness, so that, as St Paul says, though we have nothing in a worldly sense, yet spiritually we possess all things in life worth having.

✠

When we love all the world, we are conforming with the ruling Spirit of the universe. This means that instead of constantly battling against our fellow men, or against our own hatred, jealousy and violence, we are peacefully swimming with the tide. Our lives are passed in an atmosphere of warm, human love. I say 'human' advisedly, for it is this very quality which makes us human—as distinguished from the animal instincts of the survival of the fittest.

Love, joy and peace are rightly associated with one another. Life will not always be easy—we shall have our share of misfortune, illness, loss and bereavement. But beneath it all we may feel the harmony, the joy and the peace of knowing that what little value we possess is surrendered by us and submerged in the peaceful flood of God's love.

Life is like an intercepted cypher telegram. We see a lot of signs and dashes and a jumble of meaningless syllables, but we have no idea of what it all means. It just does not make any sense at all. Love alone is the key which reduces all the chaos and confusion to a plain simple message.

23 *Peace*

Peace is the basis of the interior life. Nothing is necessary in order to remain in this peace except never to depart from total self-abandonment. Nothing happens in this world but by the order of God or at least by His divine permission, and all that He permits turns infallibly to the advantage of submissive souls.

The great principle of the interior life lies in peace of the heart. The reason for this is that peace and tranquillity of spirit alone give the soul great force to achieve all that God wills. We must therefore firmly reject all that does not bear this mark of peace, submission, gentleness and confidence. The most efficacious method of interior advance is a simple acquiescence in all that God wills.

This extract from *The Spiritual Letters of Father de Caussade* is remarkable. Most of us, I think, are inclined to think wistfully of peace as some happy state to which we may some day attain as the fruit of a life devoted to selfless service. We complain of all our worries and troubles and we sigh for peace to be granted to us. But de Caussade's approach is different. He says that we ourselves must take peace by realizing that nothing can happen to us without God's approval. It is well to remember that Christ himself spoke to his disciples of peace an hour or two before his passion. His peace was not affected by outward circumstances but was the product of his interior dependence on God.

De Caussade speaks of peace as the first step in a life

of service. Yet perhaps I am mistaken in such a statement, because he claims that peace is the result of total self-surrender to God—a state which may take a long time to achieve. Nevertheless, he does approach the question from an original angle, because he states that peace is something that we must actively achieve, not an idyllic condition which will somehow be bestowed on us.

Let us therefore begin this chapter with the action which he alleges to be the essential pre-condition of peace—total self-abandonment. The incessant activities of our senses, seeing, hearing and feeling, keep our minds occupied for most of the day with our own desires, pleasures and distresses. Most of the world around us lives in the same manner, sometimes exhilarated and sometimes depressed, engrossed in outside events and in the passing circumstances of each day.

If, however, we pause and make the effort to think, we can realize that to live our lives under the sole influence of quickly passing events is scarcely a worthy use to make of the only life on this earth which, as far as we know, we shall ever live. Nor is it a happy one. For if we try to make it tolerable by seeking passing pleasures, it only seems the more dreary when the pleasures go wrong. Moreover living at the mercy of passing events requires, to be bearable, a fairly good state of health, with the result that illness or pain plunges us into depression. And our preoccupation is not only with passing daily events, for we are haunted also by anxieties for the future, by fears of losing our work, our money or our health—fears of public upheavals or of the state of the world. Most of the Western world today lives in this restless, uneasy, superficial manner.

Self-abandonment to God means the realization that all these things are not what really matters; that nothing happens in this world but by the order of God, and that every event is sent to strengthen our characters and our courage. In a sense, therefore, we may say that belief is the essential foundation of interior peace. This does not mean belief in abstruse points of dogma, but belief that everything which happens to us is sent by God for our good.

If we are satisfied that God is in control and that everything which can befall us is sent by him, then we cannot possibly allow ourselves to be depressed by our little daily troubles and reverses, for we know that they are sent to us in love. We ought to be glad of the opportunity to show our Father that we can rise to the tests that he sets us. 'Count it all joy when ye fall into divers temptations,' says James in his letter. The Standard Revised Version translates this passage: 'Count it all joy, my brethren, when you meet various trials, for you know that the testing of your faith produces steadfastness.'

Obviously the belief that everything that happens is sent by God should also abolish our fears for the future, for anything that can possibly occur will have received the approval of our Father in advance. In any case there is nothing we can do to prevent trials and temptations from coming, our anxious fears and forebodings are useless and only wear us out. But, it may be argued, things do not always just happen. We may be faced with a threatening situation, and be called upon to take a decision in advance. How can we avoid anxiety in such a possible crisis?

Firstly let us remember that we were speaking of peace of mind, which does not mean passivity or mere sitting back and letting matters drift. Of course we must act and make our decisions. But this *should* not destroy our peace of mind, for we must decide what to do without worrying. How can we decide between two alternatives without worrying which to choose? This is perhaps where lies the crux of self-abandonment. If we have truly dedicated ourselves to God's service, we must base our decision solely and completely on God's will. Doubters may ask how we know God's will. The most obvious method is to ask him. Most probably we shall be answered by ourselves thinking of a solution which God has placed in our minds. We shall not hear a clap of thunder or a voice from heaven, but the best course will just occur to us. As we have already seen, there is no reason to doubt that God can put ideas in our minds, as it were by extra-sensory perception.

There is of course no objection to using 'common sense', which in fact may be God's answer, on condition that we do not interpret as common sense our own material advantage. We must use our intelligence to choose what seems to be right, not what will be profitable to ourselves, or give us the least trouble. We may also seek guidance from the Bible, from religious books, or by consulting other persons who are themselves seeking to serve God. From the point of view of self-dedication, however, the whole point is that we must completely and without mental reservations choose what we believe to be God's will, regardless of our private inclinations. If we do this, we shall retain our peace of mind. If we have honestly tried to serve God and our decision is mistaken, he will not blame us.

✠

All this has perhaps been made to sound too simple. We choose carefully the course which seems to be the right one. But this assumes that all our emotions are completely under our control. Unfortunately they usually are not. We cannot avoid being agitated, depressed and afraid. We find it almost impossible to avoid giving our decision a slight push to one side or the other, in accordance with our own wishes, prejudices or fears. Success therefore depends on our power to restrain our own desires and anxieties and *really* to subordinate them to God's will. To acquire this power may require long years of training.

The account of the passion, as related in the gospels, offers us both guidance and encouragement. We need not be reduced to despair by our weakness, for we see that even Christ himself was afraid. 'Being in an agony He prayed more earnestly,' writes St Luke. 'Yet learned He obedience by the things which He suffered,' we are told in Hebrews 5. This seems to confirm that suffering is sent to teach us and that even Christ himself suffered intensely.

The account of the passion gives us our clearest lesson on suffering. For though our Lord went through a period during which he was in an agony of fear, he still said: 'Father, if it be possible let this cup pass from me; nevertheless not as I will, but as Thou wilt.' And he prayed the second time: 'Father, if this cup may not pass way from me, except I drink it, Thy will be done' (Matthew 26). This is our perfect example of self-abandonment.

It is also our most perfect example of peace. For no sooner was his victory won over the agony of anticipation, than he said quietly to the disciples, 'Rise, let us be going.' A few minutes later a great multitude poured into the quiet olive grove. Armed with swords and staves, the rough crowd surrounded him, holding up flaring torches. But by now his battle had been won. He was calm, collected and in complete control of the situation. He asked, 'Whom seek ye?' and they answered him, 'Jesus of Nazareth'. He answered them quietly, 'I am he'.

It is worth noting that, until the very last moment, he could have escaped. Behind the Mount of Olives the ground falls away steeply in wild, uninhabited rocky slopes, cliffs and ravines to the Jordan valley, beyond which lay the district of Peraea, which was outside the jurisdiction of the High Priest and the Sanhedrin. This was before the days of the telephone to alert the police in the Jordan valley. It was dark and the temple police carried only smoky torches. He could easily have slipped away down the rocky mountainside. But his moral battle was over and his soul was at peace.

At the last supper, before his ordeal had commenced, he had told the disciples that he gave them peace. Their minds were not to be worried, nor were they to be afraid. Now he put his own teaching into practice before their very eyes. For the ensuing seventeen or eighteen hours, filled with hatred, violence, abuse, flogging, torture and unimaginable horror, he remained calm and at peace. This is surely our supreme example. Once the surrender is made, once we have abandoned ourselves to God, we can remain in peace of mind and rise calm and victorious above all the trials, agonies and disasters which the outside world can heap upon us.

With this example before them, the authors of the New Testament never cease to return to the theme of peace. To appreciate the meaning of the emphasis which they lay on peace, we must remember the conditions under which they lived and the brutal background of their lives. Everywhere the Christians were mobbed and hunted, beaten in the streets, flogged by the authorities, thrown into prison, and chased from city to city with unrelenting vindictiveness. Nearly all the prominent men in the movement were executed, many with torture.

It was against this kind of background that references to peace in the New Testament were written after the passion and the resurrection of Christ. Here are a few, chosen at random:

> Preaching peace by Jesus Christ; He is Lord of all.
>
> Peace from God our Father and the Lord Jesus Christ.
>
> Being justified by faith, we have peace with God.

> To be spiritually minded is life and peace.
>
> The kingdom of God is righteousness and peace and joy . . . Let us therefore follow after the things that make for peace.
>
> The God of hope fill you with all joy and peace.
>
> God hath called us to peace. God is not the author of confusion but of peace.
>
> The fruit of the Spirit is love, joy, peace, long-suffering, gentleness, goodness, faith.

There are many more in the same vein.

It is noticeable that in the New Testament the word joy is continually associated with peace. Perhaps this is to be expected, for it is our anxieties regarding our worldly interests which destroy our peace of mind and our happiness. Total self-giving to God may therefore be expected to remove the earthly worries which destroy our peace. But joy is something more positive than a mere lack of anxiety. It is produced by the knowledge that we are serving Somebody who loves us and whom we love. This joy can be bubbling up in our souls like the living water of which Christ spoke to the Samaritan woman—'the water that I shall give him shall be in him a well of water, springing up into everlasting life'.

Here are some familiar references to joy taken from the New Testament. 'That my joy might remain in you, and that your joy might be full' (John 15.11). 'Your sorrow shall be turned into joy.' 'Your joy no man taketh from you.' 'The disciples were filled with joy.' 'The kingdom of God is joy.' 'The God of hope fill you with all joy.' 'The fruit of the Spirit is love, joy and peace,' and many others in the same strain. There can be no doubt whatever that the duty of every Christian is to rejoice and to praise God. For our rejoicing is not dependent on money or on politics, but on the knowledge that God is Love, that he controls the world and that he knows and is concerned for each one of us. Here is a modern quotation from Horace Bushnell, taken from M. V. Nelson's *An Anthology of Joy*:

> Joy is for all men. It does not depend on circumstance or condition: if it did, it could only be for the few. It is not the fruit of good luck, or of fortune, or even of outward success, which all men cannot have. It is of the soul, or the soul's character: it is the wealth of the soul's whole being when it is filled with the spirit of Jesus, which is the spirit of eternal love.

24 *Of Human Freedom*

Our mission in the world is the same as it has always been, to build the Kingdom of God, which is a kingdom of love. Love cannot exist except between persons. For there to be love, we must first of all safeguard the liberty and integrity of the human person.

(Thomas Merton, *The Power and Meaning of Love*)

Let us once again remind ourselves why God must necessarily be love. The reason is that no action can lead to moral progress if it is carried out under compulsion or out of fear or from hope of personal gain. If therefore God wishes to raise the human race to higher moral levels, he can only do so with the consent of the men and women involved. How can their consent be won? Only by his leadership—only if he can draw them by love voluntarily to obey his commandments.

But, it may be objected, God is all-powerful. How can we say that he can only change men and women with their consent? Of course, God *is* all-powerful. He could compel human beings to abandon wickedness, by killing all those who did not obey. But he does not only wish to prevent people from stealing and killing. He wishes them to become his children by growing more like him. He could compel us to abstain from certain actions but this process would not make us grow more like him and become his children. Fear may produce outward obedience but it cannot win love.

Human authorities can secure outward obedience to their orders by using compulsion. But it is not our external acts but our internal attitudes and affections which must be changed if we are to draw nearer to God. He, as we have seen, can gradually remould our characters if we are willing, by passing ideas into our minds, but this can only be done to individuals. The kingdom, Christ explained, was within each one of us.

Speaking to Nicodemus, he said emphatically, 'Verily, verily, I say unto thee, except a man be born again he cannot see the kingdom of God.' Nicodemus seems at first to take the statement to mean literally physical rebirth. But our Lord explains that he is referring to a spiritual rebirth, a complete re-orientation of the objects of our lives: 'That which is born of the flesh is flesh, and that which is born of the Spirit is spirit.' However, it may be noted in passing that those who have no contact with the Spirit cannot even *see* the kingdom of God. This is the condition in which most of us pass our lives. We are surrounded and overwhelmed by the turmoil and stress of the material world, and we just do not *see* anything beyond it.

All through the Gospels we find Christ speaking to individuals one by one, healing them or giving them spiritual advice. He never tried to organize a mass movement. We may perhaps think that this is too slow a way to convert the world. But we do not know whether Christ visualized such an objective. Those who had been born again were to be the salt of the earth, a seasoning, a light visible to others, a little flock. He even expressed doubt whether, at his second coming, he would find faith on the earth.

We like to picture a coming millennium, when the whole human race will be dedicated to God's service, but we cannot be sure if this will occur. Neither Christ nor the Bible tells us the whole of God's plan. Doubtless it would be far beyond our comprehension. We are only told what it is necessary for us to know.

But the trouble which our Lord took to deal with

persons, immensely enhances the value of every individual human soul. It undoubtedly means that every separate human soul must establish its private contact with the Spirit if it is to live a life in the service of God. Once the soul has been reborn—has turned its back on the madding struggle of the material world and is facing towards the world of spirit—then God himself will come and live in it and will give it the guidance and the strength to grow. The whole process is an individual one between every separate soul and the Spirit of God. There is thus no means of raising the moral standards of the human race and of leading it to co-operate with God except by individual conversions. These can only be achieved by love and not by laws or compulsion.

It is possible nowadays for speakers to obtain a much wider audience than was the case in the time of our Lord. With public-address loudspeaker equipment, an evangelist may be heard by many thousands of people. Radio or television can command even larger audiences. An increasing number of persons in the world can read and write, and books and newspapers can reach ever wider audiences. Yet these mass means of evangelization can only serve to awake the interest or the attention of the audience. After each session of Dr Billy Graham's evangelization crusades, those interested are asked to come forward and are passed on to individual counsellors to learn more. Every individual must sooner or later make his or her own decision whether to continue absorbed in the daily struggle for material objects, or whether to turn about and to seek guidance from the Spirit as to how they may devote their lives to the service of God and their neighbours.

While, however, greater facilities for the circulation of literature and for the hearing of the human voice may have assisted evangelists in drawing the attention of people to the existence of God, the same changes have acted even more powerfully in the opposite direction. For most of the public media operate for profit and are therefore inclined to tell people what they want to hear rather than the truth.

More subtle still, however, is their dulling effect on individual thought. Simple people all over the world are faced with the conditions of human life—with poverty, cold, sickness, parting, bereavement and death. The sorrows and the suffering which they see about them can inspire their quiet thoughts to ponder on God and human life. But great numbers of people today never pause to think at all. On the way to work in the morning, they read the paper. Returning from work in the evening, they switch on the television. All day long they are bombarded by other people's thoughts mostly directed to amusing them with a view to taking their money. Everything is noisy, exciting and completely superficial. The deep things of life, the existence of God, the object of human life, the inevitability of death are excluded from ever entering their minds.

'The test of leadership,' wrote John Buchan, 'is not to put greatness into humanity but to elicit it, for the greatness is already there.' But the public media which fill our thoughts today do not awaken and draw out our greatness. They smother it with a torrent of frivolity, malice and materialism. It is not necessary for the media to be wicked or immoral in order to counteract the divine spark in every human being. They can stifle the greatness which is latent in every human soul with a flood of superficialities.

We can, by contrast, understand that Christ taught the priceless value of every single human soul. Every individual, he said, must be born again, must voluntarily and consciously face its own problems, abandon its absorption in the material world, and realize the existence of the spiritual world. God's spirit would then enter it and guide it.

A society which has abandoned individual thought regarding the deeper things of life, and has grown accustomed to accept other people's ideas without thinking, is in a situation of great danger. It is at the mercy of any person or party which can control the public media. Such a situation makes it possible for whole nations to be whipped up into fanatical enthusiasm by those who have the power to disseminate their thoughts to people who never think for themselves.

Another factor here enters into the situation. Our minds have been entirely flooded with thoughts of the external world, we are also constantly reminded of the amazing discoveries which we have made in the material world in the last fifty years. We are taught to despise the history of the human race through its thousands of years. *They* did not have televisions, or jet aircraft or nuclear weapons. We are thus led to the conclusion that we are the greatest people who ever existed, and that with our brilliant intellects we can create an earthly paradise. Pride comes before a fall—arrogance is a potentially fatal disease.

✠

The result of our intellectual arrogance is the belief that man can save himself by his own cleverness. Any mention of the spiritual world is scornfully rejected as an old myth. To create his ideal world man can employ science, technology, finance, coercion, weapons and war. Different groups draw up their own plans for the ideal society, and inaugurate mass movements to bring in their golden age. The party line soon becomes for them the solution to every problem. The policy of the party becomes sacrosanct, to the complete neglect of the individual human being. All human feeling and all personal relationships—all respect for love, compassion or human kindness—are abrogated. Any man who dares to oppose the party line is regarded as a public enemy. The mass fury of the party is turned against him. Where the process is carried to extremes, it is essential that the members are not allowed to think. Otherwise they might have ideas contrary to the party line. As a result there soon appears mob violence against dissidents, then the concentration camp, the labour camp and the gas chamber.

To maintain the party at red heat an enemy is necessary, to whom all the evils of the time or the failures of the party can be attributed. The enemy is endlessly denounced in savage propaganda and in violent speeches by the leaders. Hate is the fuel which keeps the party working and fighting with the driving force of fanaticism. Anyone will suffice for an enemy—the Versailles Treaty Powers, the Jews, capitalism, imperialism (or any other -ism)—to which all the hardships of the masses can be attributed.

Communism, Fascism and Nazism were totalitarian mass movements of this kind, founded on hate. Some people believe Communism and Nazism to be opposites, but this is only a superficial illusion. Both were similar phenomena, mass movements built on hate and completely destructive of human personality and of human freedom.

There were strong Christian communities in both Germany and Russia. I used to wonder why the Nazis and the Communists alike persecuted these loyal and patriotic sections of their populations. But the explanation is now obvious—their bitter hostility was automatic and inevitable. For to Christianity every human soul is of priceless value, for only human individuals can love. Personal freedom is the necessary preliminary to every moral action, to every dedicated act of service. A fanatical mob can be stirred to a frenzy of hatred and destruction, but not to love. If the party were invaded by love it would break up, and each individual would turn to his neighbour to help him.

Numbers of people in every country are discontented or frustrated and are unable to face life alone. Such people readily fall in with a fanatical mass movement, based on hate. The futility of their own lives can be blamed on the enemy. Membership of the party gives them a feeling of power and importance. They are freed from the responsibility of taking their own decisions. By blindly adhering to the party line, they can commit cruelties without any qualms of conscience. Revelling in the power of the party, they are freed from their personal feelings of inferiority and helplessness.

Eventually the mad fanaticism runs out of steam, but the leaders have meanwhile established an iron grip on the nation, which is ultimately subjected to a ruthless despotism far more autocratic and cruel than that of the original society from which the party had claimed to free it.

Man-made plans for the ideal society can never agree. A rival group using the same methods propounds an alternative Utopia. The two mass movements clash in a frenzied struggle of terrorism or of war, as did the Communists and the Nazis. As long as we arrogantly believe that human planning can produce Utopia, we shall be torn by fighting and terror, for human planners never agree. Only when all parties bow to what they admit to be the superhuman commands of God can sufficient common ground be found to enable them to live at peace.

Of course there have always been periodic wild outbursts of fanaticism and savagery in the world. But the dangers which they create and the areas to which they can spread have been immensely increased by modern methods of propaganda, by the press, the radio and television, and by the increasing but elementary literacy of the masses.

✠

Socialism is an elastic term which can mean anything or

nothing and may consequently be misleading. The iron tyranny of communist Russia claims to be socialism, as do the mildest ideals of the Fabians. The immense majority of the people of Britain are moderate, good-tempered and benevolent. These qualities do not, however, entirely exempt them from the attractions of party membership. The danger arises when the policy of the party is deemed to be sacred, and party discipline is set up to enforce it. The same applies to trade unions, which aspire to discipline members who hold opinions which do not accord with the policy of the union. Here are the first beginnings of the destruction of human freedom. The trade unions have not yet established concentration camps, but they can deprive workers of their employment and of the means of supporting their families.

All human beings have the virtues of loyalty and comradeship planted in their souls. The most insidious propaganda is that which depicts obedience to the party or the union as loyalty to comrades, for it uses human virtues to deprive people of their freedom. Mass movements want members who have surrendered their God-given power of Free Will though they may not be aware of the fact. Christianity recognizes the priceless value of every human soul and cannot approve of mass movements consisting of human cyphers, whose opinions are dictated to them by party bosses.

The kingdom of God is the kingdom of love and is based on the freedom of every individual to exercise his or her Free Will in moral choices. A nation of free individuals can be controlled by positive leadership, that is to say by constructive love, for only individuals are open to love. This statement may seem to be a piece of impractical idealism. Certainly, such leadership will not convert the whole nation, but it will leaven the lump. There will still be criminals, men of violence, haters, whom the police will have quietly to restrain.

The essential is always to remember that God has created us with Free Will to make moral choices, a fact which requires every Christian to retain his personal freedom. In fact it does not seem to me to be any exaggeration to say that, in the modern world, Christianity is the only barrier to the establishment of totalitarianism, a fact which both Nazis and Communists fully appreciated, for, while fighting each other, both persecuted the Christians.

In Matthew 20.25–7, we read, 'The princes of the Gentiles exercise dominion over them, and they that are great exercise authority upon them. But it shall not be so among you; but whosoever will be great among you, let him be your minister: and whosoever will be chief among you, let him be your servant'—words utterly destructive of regimentation, totalitarianism and party bosses.

25 *Many Traditions but One Lord*

We have hitherto been thinking in Christian terms. But in his *Readings in St John's Gospel*, Chapter 1, the late Archbishop Temple has the following passage:

> From the beginning the divine light has shone. Always it was coming into the world; always it enlightened every man alive in his reason and his conscience. Every check on animal lust felt by the primitive savage, every stimulation to a nobler life is God self-revealed within his soul ... By the word of God ... Isaiah and Plato, and Zoroaster and Buddha and Confucius conceived and uttered such truths as they declared. There is only one divine light; and every man in his measure is enlightened by it.

God has always guided men unknown to themselves. His inspiration has been the unseen cause of every upward step in human morals. But the narrow-mindedness of men has prevented them from seeing the divine messages received by other peoples. Rather have they seen them as rivals to their own revelations.

The archbishop continues:

> Yet this light is not recognized for what it is. If it were, its fuller shining would always be welcomed. But it is attributed by each tribe or group to some historic or legendary founder or pioneer of their own, so that each claims to have a monopoly of the light itself, when in fact each has only a few rays of that light. It has to shine through veils of prejudice and obsession, so that even the rays received by each group among mankind are not

clear and pure in the illumination which they give.

So the light is unrecognized; and when it blazes out more fully, men refuse it, even though it is that by which they already walk.

If God wishes to raise us to higher moral levels so that we can communicate with him, is it reasonable to suppose that he wishes to draw only Christians to himself? And what did he feel for the human race in the ages before Christ appeared on earth? Was he then concerned only with the Children of Israel? And was he indifferent to his own creatures before the birth of Abraham?

Little as we can understand in this life, it does seem more reasonable to suppose that he created all men and has always regarded them all with sympathy and affection. But if he chose the human species to be raised to communion with himself, we have already seen that they have to rise through their own efforts and through their own moral choices. This would require a long and gradual process. He could perhaps have transformed us into angels by a wave of his wand, but in that case we would not have become moral personalities.

It accordingly seems to me reasonable to believe that God has always guided the human race by inserting ideas into their minds. In the early stages, these ideas would be extremely simple, as in the early books of the Old Testament, gradually developing into higher morality and the promptings of duty and love.

But here intervenes the pathetic smallness of the human mind, to which we are obliged constantly to return. Each slight revelation of God's word is claimed by some group as its private property, and the person to whom the revelation came is hailed as the greatest teacher of all time. Even when a higher revelation later appears, it is rejected in favour of the earlier teacher who belonged to their own group.

The Jewish rejection of the incarnate Christ is the example which most readily comes to mind. Fondly and proudly attached as they were to their old traditions, the Jews could not accept an even higher revelation, which transformed their rules and regulations into a covenant of love. Christ himself expressed the situation in a nutshell when he assured them that he had not come to destroy but to fulfill—to carry their old revelation a step higher.

Such thoughts as these tend to modify our attitude to others. A hundred years ago, Christian missionaries often approached the adherents of other religions by telling them that they must abandon their old traditions and begin all over again by believing in Jesus Christ. But if all spiritual and moral progress is infused into human beings by God, this approach would seem to have been erroneous.

We are entitled to see our own religion as embodying higher moral standards than do other religions, but what if they also were originally revealed by the same God? Moreover humility is a basic Christian virtue, for it embodies our own realization that we are all as nothing before God. An arrogant approach—I am entirely right and you are entirely wrong—serves only to arouse human resentment rather than to call forth sympathy and affection.

Charles de Foucauld, who lived alone in the Sahara, showed a more Christian approach. He did not count up the number of his converts. He believed that the true way to convert was so to live our lives that others would come to us and ask us for our secret. He never made a convert nor was he ever joined by an associate. But now, sixty years after his death, the Little Brothers and Sisters of Jesus, the order which he founded, is scattered all over the world. The lesson is that we can never judge and should not concern ourselves with the results of our work. 'The extraordinary thing is that God uses us, who are so insignificant,' writes Carlo Carretto, one of Charles de Foucauld's Little Brothers of Jesus.

The heritage of Western prejudice often makes Europeans think of Arabs as violent and fanatical. My many years in close intimacy with Muslim communities did not confirm these prejudices. On the contrary I found them more warm-hearted than Europeans. They seemed to me to be more fond of children and in general more welcoming, more pleasant and more hospitable.

The people whom today we call Arabs are of many different ethnic origins, but all those I have encountered seemed to possess something of these characteristics. It would seem therefore that part at least of these lovable qualities must be attributed to their Muslim background. Indeed I have known Muslim saints who showed the same qualities of gentleness and renunciation of the world, which we associate with Christianity.

The simpler Arabs feel no embarrassment in speaking of religion. Arab N.C.O.s and soldiers have often spoken to me deprecating a particular action, on the grounds that it would not be acceptable to God. Muslims sometimes put modern Western Christians to shame in the practice of praising God. Their speech is still filled with pious interjections, 'If God wills', and 'Praise be to God'. Much of this is now perhaps only social convention, but nevertheless a considerable residue of piety still permeates the daily conversation of most Muslims.

The attitude of tolerance to and co-operation with other religions is not a purely modern development. William Law (1686–1761) wrote in his book, *The Spirit of Prayer*:

> There is but one salvation for all mankind, and that is the life of God in the soul. God has but one design or intent towards all mankind and that is to introduce or generate His own Life, Light and Spirit in them ...

There is but one possible way for man to attain this salvation, or Life of God in the soul. There is not one for the Jew, another for a Christian and a third for the heathen. No; God is one, human nature is one, salvation is one and the way to it is one.

✲

Propaganda, that great modern machine for the production of hate, labours all to often to draw an unfavourable picture of other races and communities. We all live with bitter prejudices and thereby, all day long, we add unintentionally to the hatreds and the violence which dominate our world.

Human affairs, however, are complicated, and sweeping generalizations are usually misleading. We cannot say that the simple manners of Arab villagers are solely due to Islam, because the more sophisticated and Western-educated Arabs do not show these qualities in so marked a degree. In the same manner in the Western nations, country people may be more earnest Christians than are the inhabitants of cities. In every country, education and external factors may influence the attitude of the people to religion.

When I was in Jordan, I became interested in the town of Kerak, the Kir Moab of the Old Testament, which had also been a Crusader fortress. The inhabitants were partly Christian and partly Muslim, but both communities lived together in close cordiality. Before the First World War, they shared the same building for worship, the Muslims using it for prayers on Fridays, and the Christians on Sundays.

It used to be said that old persons nearing death would often join both religions. Differences in intellectual beliefs were puzzling and it would be unfortunate to be consigned to hell for having made a mistake in choosing between them. So it seemed to be safer to be both a Muslim and a Christian at the same time. This happy ecumenism was only disturbed by the arrival of Western missionaries, who not only protested against co-operation with Muslims, but who succeeded in converting some of the local Orthodox Christians to become Roman Catholics, Baptists or Seventh Day Adventists. Yet something of the old feeling remained—the Roman Catholic priest appointed to the town, an Irishman, used to say that Islam was only a Christian heresy.

When considering any questions of religion, it is essential clearly to differentiate between two types of people. Firstly those who are called by one religious label or another, merely because they were born in a country or a community which supposedly professed that religion. Secondly, those who take their religion seriously and earnestly endeavour to live up to it. Intentional or thoughtless confusion between the two classes leads to endless misunderstanding and at times to premeditated hostile propaganda.

Muslims, for example, are often repelled by the low standards of sexual morality prevalent among Western nations and denounce this laxness as the result of Christianity. Yet Christ himself said that a man who even looked at a woman to lust after her committed adultery. During the Second World War, many Arabs asked me how the European powers could bomb open cities, thereby killing innocent women and children. Christianity was said to be the religion of love, so how could Christians bomb whole populations in this cruel manner?

Christians, on the other hand, have the idea that in Muslim countries women are 'mere chattels'. Superficially social systems differ, but it often seemed to me that many Muslims are more affectionate to their families than are Europeans. These are mere random examples to illustrate how actions of one kind or another in different countries are sometimes used for hostile religious propaganda, although the actions concerned may be directly contrary to the religion which the people involved are supposed to profess. It is, therefore, essential, in comparing different religions, to consider only those individuals who genuinely try to live in accordance with their religion.

If we accept that all such religions found their origins in the promptings of the Spirit of God, we find ourselves free to co-operate with and to learn from such revelations, without being charged with the betrayal of our own religious traditions.

✠

In addition, when comparing a nation of supposed Muslims, Christians or Hindus, it is also necessary to consider the non-religious mental atmosphere in which people live and which influences their total personalities and thence their conduct.

The dominant feature of Western life today is materialism. In the last fifty years, this cynical attitude to life has been seeping into the Muslim world. This process has been caused by the dominant position occupied by the Western world in the 1920s and the 1930s. Since then the many Muslims who have studied in Western universities have taken back to their countries the impression, formerly unknown to them, that the object of human life is the accumulation of wealth. These Muslim students tend to exhibit the same intellectual arrogance towards those who believe in a spiritual world as do their Western mentors.

✠

One of the factors which caused me the greatest surprise on returning to live in Britain after thirty-six years among the Arabs was the fact that our government did not consider itself responsible in any way for public morals. Soon after our arrival in England, I read with amazement an article in the press about our moral decline. The article argued that Britain was a free country and consequently, if the people desired the exhibition of films depicting sexual lust or violent crime, they were perfectly entitled to have them. This, it was claimed, was democracy. This attitude is similar to that of the slogan, 'My morals are my own affair'. We know now that this statement is completely mistaken. We are all part of one another and we all deeply influence one another.

Sexual immorality and the abandonment of the sanctity of marriage has peopled our country with neglected, disturbed and unwanted children. The alleged 'supersession' of patriotism and of sense of obligation to the community has resulted in our infliction of continual suffering on one another through lock-outs, strikes and boycotts—each group intent only on obtaining more money for themselves at the expense of their fellow countrymen. Every example of selfishness, greed or immorality of which we are guilty is another nail in the coffin of our country.

This being the case, it is surely the duty of the government to set a high moral example, and to call upon everyone to offer themselves in selfless service to their country. Many politicians unfortunately are too timid to state the facts boldly and to call for moral reform. Might not such an initiative lose votes in the next election? It is safer to let things slide and simply to promise everyone more money if they vote for us.

Our system, which we call democracy without thinking much about the meaning of the word, has completely failed to produce leaders with the courage and devotion to save the nation by giving us moral leadership. Without the guidance of moral principles, such people follow only a shortsighted opportunism, directed to catch votes.

The government of this country was not always indifferent to the moral and spiritual welfare of the nation. Three hundred years ago, it accepted responsibility not only for the people's morals but for their religious beliefs. At the opposite extreme from today's laxity, they persecuted those whose religous beliefs differed from the official creed. But we have already seen that compulsion cannot lead to moral progress, which can only be achieved by example and by constructive leadership.

As we have seen, the universe seems to be governed on this principle. God never uses force, but by the example of Christ, the saints and the prophets, and by the inspiration of his word in our souls, he leads us to a higher standard of spiritual life. By imitating his methods, we are, as it were, swimming with the tide of the universe. If our governments could set an example of morality, and could speak forcibly of our desperate need for selfless service, the result would be sensational. Perhaps, by this means, a new atmosphere of co-operation and comradeship could be produced, between all classes and callings.

Unfortunately, far from this ideal, the action of our governments has not been limited to indifference to moral issues. They have also permitted the abolition of many laws enforcing public decency. This action has not been the result of doubt of the efficacy of legislation. On the contrary, never have so many hasty and ill-digested laws been passed in so short a time.

Blasphemy, obscenity, pornography and unnatural vices had been banned by law for centuries, but are now permitted in the name of freedom and democracy. If I light a bonfire in my garden and the smoke drifts over to my neighbours, the sanitary inspector calls, wants to carry out an inquiry and warns me against polluting the neighbourhood. The prohibition of pornography and vice was intended to save my neighbours from moral pollution. Possibly such vices were always practised in secrecy, but their prohibition by law protected the public, and particularly young people, from pollution. Unaware of the existence of such practices, they were not tempted to indulge in them.

The essential fact to remember is that we are all part of one another. My morals are NOT only my own affair, they tend inevitably to purify or to pollute the whole community. I cannot be immoral, dishonest or malicious without injuring my neighbours. The greatest service we can render during our brief earthly lives is not to make money or to manage a big business, but simply ourselves to be devoted and selfless.

Such Muslim governments as I have served were, to a varying degree, conscious of their obligation to protect public morality. The slow seepage of Western ideas into Muslim leaders may, however, weaken their concern for this duty in the future.

✠

Perhaps we have now said enough to enable us to see how we should behave towards other religions. It seems to me unfortunate that so many religions lay emphasis on belief in certain alleged facts. In my intimate relationships with many Muslims, I naturally avoided the discussion of specific beliefs over which our two religions differed. But this left an immense open field for the discussion of a way of life which would be pleasing to God.

Let us then remember that almost all religions have probably originated in some divine revelation. But the universal narrow-mindedness of the human race causes us all to claim that the tiny ray of light which has reached each one of us is the only light in the universe. When we realize that all goodness comes from God, we can co-operate with members of other denominations or other religions in the task of loving God and our neighbours, which Christ said was the whole of religion.

The influence of example is the principal way in which the saints have changed the world. 'The man in the street does not read the Bible, he reads us.' 'It is by knowing *us* that men are to be saved,' said William Temple . . . 'It is not by what we say that we are good pastors, nor by what we do, but by what we *are*'. When we have realized this, we have discovered a worthwhile purpose for our lives.

There are, however, in my opinion, two courses which are to avoided. The first is the rather dilettante dabbling in or ostensible conversion to some other (usually oriental) cult. 'Christianity has failed,' such people announce, 'so I am trying Yoga or have become a Buddhist.' In fact, Christianity has not failed but we have failed to abandon ourselves to it. Full participation in any other religion requires self-surrender as does Christianity.

At first it seems exciting to practise oriental meditation, but these various traditions stretch back through thousands of years. We cannot change our spiritual heritage overnight as we change our coats. If we have failed to be good Christians we are not likely to become saintly Hindus.

A second course which I think is mistaken is the idea of a synthetic religion. Why not adopt the transmigration of souls into our beliefs or the maxims of Confucius? The essential factor in all religions, however, is not the facts of belief or the speculations for the future, but total and selfless dedication to God and our neighbour now.

The Western nations, and especially the U.S.A., has, ever since President Woodrow Wilson in 1918, clung to the rather arrogant idea that all mankind can be made like us almost overnight. Are we right in our petty conceit to think that all men should be like us?

Someone (was it Winston Churchill?) has said that the West has talked itself into decadence. The study of comparative religions is often not religious at all, but another subject on which clever people can talk, write and debate.

26 *Soldiers*

It may seem curious to include a chapter on soldiers in a book which is intended to be devoted to the service of God and man. I have been a soldier all my life and at heart I am still a lover of soldiering. Nowadays, especially I think in Britain, many people visualize soldiers as a class of brutal men who enjoy killing people. 'Surely you cannot be a Christian if you are a soldier,' a young man said to me recently. I am concerned to put forward another viewpoint of my profession.

May I then be allowed to express a personal opinion? I have always been devoted to soldiering because to me it embodied the two ideas of love and service. Soldiers are nearly always badly paid, and the accumulation of money cannot be their objective. They, with sailors and airmen, are called the Armed Services, a public recognition that they spend their lives serving others, not seeking their own interests or pleasure. In a world governed by the struggle for money and power, these are facts which merit some consideration.

Their lives indeed are self-surrendered. They cannot decide where they will go or where they will live. Their movements often involve anguished goodbyes to their families and the heartache of long separation from their wives and children. Moreover they may at any moment be exposed to danger and death, leaving widows and orphans all too scantily provided for by the parsimony of ungrateful governments. The idea that service fills a psychological need for men who are not attracted by the passion for money rarely occurs to the general public. These hardships endured by soldiers provoke little sympathy from the public, at least in Britain. 'Presumably he was too lazy or too stupid to earn an honest living in any other way,' is the kind of comment often provoked by the news that a young man has joined the army.

Some will perhaps reply, 'Well, we grant that soldiers do serve and that for a meagre reward, but how do you make out that soldiering typifies love?' I think that people who serve together in some good cause often become united by a feeling of close fellowship. This emotion is felt even by people who only come together now and again to work for some charitable cause. If the service they render occupies all their time their association is, of course, both stronger and warmer. But when their service involves real hardship, and even mortal danger, their feeling for one another is enormously intensified.

Most old soldiers would probably shy at the use of the word love, but would cordially agree that the factor which carried them through all their sufferings was comradeship. Perhaps we could compromise by using the word brotherhood—a deep affection for our companions. The history of war is full of heroic examples of the devotion of soldiers for their comrades, risking and often losing their lives in attempts to save a wounded comrade, sharing with him the last drop of water, or helping an exhausted companion to carry his equipment. But my own words may fail to carry conviction. Let us refer to higher authorities.

I find encouragement for my views in the gospels themselves. In Luke 3.14, we are told that soldiers came to John the Baptist and asked him what they should do to bring forth fruits of repentance. John did not tell them to give up their evil profession. He said to them: 'Do violence to no man, neither accuse any falsely: and be content with your wages.' The text does not explain what kind of soldiers these were—they were presumably engaged on public security duties, one of the most unpleasant tasks which soldiers can ever have to perform.

In the eighth chapter of Matthew we find the story of the Roman centurion who came to our Lord to beg for a cure for his servant, who was grievously ill. A centurion was what we should call a company commander. This officer obviously felt a deep affection for his men, causing him to go in person to seek for the Man who might heal his servant. Jesus said to him, 'I will come and heal him.' The officer humbly replied, 'I am not worthy that Thou shouldst come under my roof: but speak the word only, and my servant shall be healed . . .' When Jesus heard it, he marvelled and said to them that followed, 'Verily I say unto you, I have not found so great faith, no, not in Israel.'

As a soldier, I naturally love this story, showing the officer so solicitous for his men, and so deeply impressed by the personality of Jesus. Almost all our Lord's reproofs and denunciations were directed against the priests, the Pharisees and the Sadducees, the official leaders of the church, who considered themselves so greatly superior to the common people. (Speaking to the man who was born blind, the Pharisees said: 'Thou wast altogether born in sins, and dost thou teach US?')

The Roman centurion was not only an army officer, he was also a servant of the imperial Roman government and part of the foreign garrison in Palestine. Yet he was profoundly humble in contrast to the haughty religious leaders of the Jewish people. His faith, our Lord said, not only exceeded that of the priests but of all the people of Israel. Christ praised this soldier highly, and never even hinted that it was a pity that such a good man should follow so base a profession.

In the fifteenth chapter of Mark, we are told that when our Lord died on the cross, and 'the centurion, which stood over against him, saw that he so cried out and gave up the ghost, he said, "Truly this Man was the Son of God."' Here again we receive the impression of a serious-minded man, alert to spiritual values. It is true that, before the crufixion, the soldiers had mocked Christ, so we cannot say that all soldiers were religious. But we can, I think, claim that being a soldier was not a bar to religion.

In the tenth chapter of Acts, we are told of another pious army officer, 'Cornelius, a centurion of the band called the Italian band, a devout man and one that feared God with all his house, which gave much alms to the people and prayed to God always.' Cornelius saw a vision in which he was told to send for Peter. He accordingly sent 'a devout soldier' to invite him. Meanwhile Peter himself had a dream in which he thought that he was invited to eat food which was ritually unclean according to the Mosaic law. When he protested, he was told 'what God hath cleansed, that call not thou common'—incidentally a useful verse to remember to check our many snobberies. Perhaps the same prohibition might be applicable to those who condemn soldiers.

Peter accordingly went with the soldier to the house of Cornelius, where he found that many people had collected to hear him. He proceeded to address the meeting and told them about Jesus. 'While Peter yet spake these words, the Holy Ghost fell on all of them which heard the word ... and they heard them speak with tongues and magnify God.' (The fact that speaking in tongues has in our own time once more become common makes this story even more vivid.) Then Peter commanded them to be baptized in the name of the Lord Jesus. The first non-Jew to receive the Holy Spirit and be baptized in the name of Christ was a Roman army officer.

The early Christians continued the gospel tradition of recognition that a soldier's life was devoted to service. Paul in his second letter to Timothy admonishes him; 'Thou, therefore, endure hardness, as a good soldier of Jesus Christ.' He would scarcely have used such a metaphor if soldiering had been regarded as a disgraceful profession, or a negation of Christianity. Again in the sixth chapter of Ephesians Paul makes use of military metaphors to describe the Christian life. 'Put on the whole armour of God, that ye may be able to stand ... Stand therefore ... having on the breastplate of righteousness ...' This tradition of comparing the Christian life to military service has been continued all down the centuries, as witness some of our most popular hymns, such as 'Onward Christian Soldiers', 'Soldiers of Christ Arise' and many more.

It may be objected that in a previous chapter we were told that Christ never consented to use violence, and that God himself draws us by love and never by compulsion. We can doubtless accept it as an axiom that we should never use violence in our own interest. Perhaps we could extend the prohibition to other forms of compulsion such as lock-outs, strikes, boycotts or economic sanctions. All such methods inflict suffering on others—usually on the innocent. Probably in nine cases out of ten better solutions could be reached by tolerance and co-operation. These principles may be applied to nations as much as to individuals.

These prohibitions, however, apply to attempts to gain money, power or advantages for ourselves or for the group, organization or nation to which we belong. The problem arises when third parties are involved. What would be our duty if we came across a man torturing a child or, on a lonely stretch of road, a man murdering a woman? Would it be our Christian duty to stand and look on at the crime, exhorting the criminal to abstain from violence and to love his enemies?

Few people will maintain such a view. Surely, where it was a question of protecting the weak, it would be our duty to throw ourselves on the aggressor with all our strength and to attempt to rescue the victim at no matter what risk to ourselves. This is the epitome of the soldier's duty—to give his life to protect the weak and the helpless. We do not know the origin of evil but we can see its activities around us all the time. As long as there are cruel, greedy and aggressive criminals at large, it is our duty to protect the defenceless, if necessary by force.

The same principles apply to nations. It is the duty of rulers and statesmen to avoid head-on collisions between nations, leading to war. Every day we see that the world still contains many governments who are desirous of increasing their own wealth and power by attacking other countries. I say governments advisedly, for the people of all nations are almost always opposed to war. To neglect our soldiers, sailors and airmen in order to improve our own social amenities is a disregard of our duty to protect the weak.

Once we recognize—and we cannot doubt it—that there are aggressive powers who wish to conquer the weak by violence, then we do not set an example for peace by abolishing or reducing our armed forces, any more than we would reduce the number of criminals by abolishing the police. Is it not our duty as a nation to maintain as strong armed forces as we can, while letting it be known that they will never be used for our own aggrandizement, but only in defence to protect the weak? To starve our own forces or to treat them with hostility or contempt is only to encourage the aggressors to bully the weak.

Marshal Lyautey of France used to say that it is wise to show force in order not to be obliged to use it. Thus the principal use of British forces in the world should be as a deterrent. Such is the way of this imperfect world that nobody pays any attention to the weak. If the voice of Britain is to carry any influence in support of peace, toleration and good government, she must be known to be strong. The decision when, if ever, to use armed force against another nation rests not with the soldiers but with the statesmen.

✠

Let us now abandon historical considerations and consider our situation today. The whole basis and spirit of Christianity is the refusal to use violence, as Christ himself refused, and he told us to love our enemies. Yet he never condemned soldiers or called for the disbandment of armies. Was this attitude paradoxical? Some Christians today seem to think so, for they demand the unilateral disarmament of our country, and refuse to serve in the forces, claiming to be conscientious objectors.

Christ did not draw up detailed orders for public life, doubtless because conditions have varied so much down the ages and in different countries that rigid orders would not long have remained applicable. He lived his life as an example to mankind and left us to apply his principles to our particular circumstances. He knew what was in man and he fully realized that the world contained many men addicted to violence and cruelty. He realized that criminals must at times be restrained by force, if ordinary people were to live in love and peace.

Paul, and other New Testament writers, appreciated the duty of supporting the authorities, even if they were pagan. In the second chapter of his first letter to Timothy, he wrote: 'I exhort, therefore, that first of all, supplications, prayers, intercessions and giving of thanks, be made for all men: for kings and for all that are in authority: that we may lead a quiet and peaceable life in all godliness and honesty; for this is good and acceptable in the sight of God our Saviour.'

Those in authority for whom Paul wished prayers to be offered were, among others, the Roman imperial officials. Today, as we have seen, there are some Christians who actually advocate violence against the authority of officials in certain countries. Such an attitude cannot be justified from the New Testament. Yet Christianity, by these methods and by the patient endurance of persecution, actually conquered the Roman Empire. When Paul asked for prayers for the authorities, he was, of course, aware that these officers maintained their authority by the use of soldiers.

But one fact emerges plainly from Christ's orders to love our enemies, though he never spoke disparagingly of soldiers. The fact is that force, when used, must never be supported by hatred but always by love. This, more than anything else, is the lesson we need to learn today. Some nationalist or revolutionary movements in many parts of the world make open use of hate to increase the fanaticism of their followers. Such an attitude is completely unchristian.

In both World Wars, and even in the Cold War, self-styled civilized nations have indulged in hatred. On the conclusion of the wars, the victors have shown the same vindictive passions in dictating the peace. It is sad to think how much wiser we were after the Napoleonic Wars, when France was immediately accepted as an equal, not loaded with vindictive penalties. Far from progressing, the world seems to be deteriorating, where the command to love our enemies is concerned.

✠

It may be argued that a soldier is committed to serve the government and that the government might initiate an unjust war. In theory this is true. But I do not think that there is any likelihood of such an occurrence nowdays in so far as Britain is concerned. The British government is more likely to starve its armed forces of weapons and money, and then to find itself unwillingly involved in hostilities, in which its inadequately equipped armed forces would die as martyrs to their duty. I believe that, in Britain at least, the traditions of Christian knighthood still survive, and that many of her soldiers feel themselves dedicated to the defence of the right and the protection of the weak.

27 *The Rising Tide of Brutality*

The animal side of human nature has always been savage. The most striking characteristic of the human race, however, is that, against this animal brutality, there have always been men and women ready to serve, to give and not to grab—people who felt that sympathy, mutual help, selflessness and love were greater than military conquest.

The First World War was fought with courage and perseverance for a noble aim. The idea prevailing at the time was that it would be the last war in history, the final defeat of militarism and aggression. Unfortunately victory proved a heady wine. The victors vented their resentments on the defeated, and thereby sowed the seeds of a Second World War.

The second war was less idealistic than the first, but its most distinguishing feature was that the development of air warfare abolished the old limitation of war to soldiers. The wholesale bombing of open cities transformed war into genocide, culminating in the final horror of Hiroshima. The same principles were continued in Vietnam and, on a smaller scale, by Israel. War had been totally changed by the proliferation of mass lethal weapons. As a result, the objective in war was no longer to defeat the enemy's army, but to attack if not to exterminate the enemy nation, man, woman and child.

The, perhaps unconscious, impression produced on the world was that of the unimportance of human life. Christianity had always claimed that every single human being possessed a soul created by God. As God had made, so God alone possessed the right to terminate human life.

Modern man is perhaps no more savage than the cave

man, but his animal side is no less so. With astonishing rapidity in the last forty years we have grown accustomed to a purely utilitarian attitude. Abortion may be used if the birth of the child would be inconvenient. Euthanasia is discussed for old people to spare them pain or perhaps to ease the relatives of trouble. Whatever the motive, human life is no longer sacred. Yet, strangely enough, while we have become so indifferent to the destruction of innocent lives, we have abolished capital punishment of criminals.

The same mental atmosphere governs the growth of terrorism. Those who advocate political, social or international changes seek to attain their objectives by depriving innocent persons of their lives. The ever increasing use of time bombs or mines, to kill anyone who happens to be passing by, is a new high-water mark of savagery. The victims are not enemies; they may well be supporters of the terrorists themselves or, more likely, innocent men, women or children, who are trying to live their ordinary lives and keep out of trouble.

The present constant dissemination of news only increases our insensitiveness. There does not seem to be any necessity why we should every few hours be told of all the crimes and disasters all over the world. There can be no doubt that the dissemination of reports describing crimes, terrorist actions, kidnappings and hijackings gives ideas to other potential criminals all over the world. But a secondary result of the broadcasting of accounts of violent crime is that we ourselves become hardened and indifferent.

Few people in Britain or the United States have, as yet, witnessed the mass murders of civilian populations or the terror-struck flight of anguished refugees driven from their homes. We read almost with indifference of the deaths or evictions of harmless civilians, women and children in South East Asia, Africa or the Middle East. Indeed the industrialized nations make financial profits and support their own armament industries by selling the weapons which enable these atrocities and massacres to continue. Often they use these savage methods to extend their own influence by supplying lethal weapons to one side or the other in the increasingly bitter and cruel local wars in Asia or Africa.

✠

We may start our consideration of this problem by realizing that the vast majority of people in every country in the world desires only to live in peace and to be left alone. It is principally governments which stir up the troubles of the world. This is largely the result of inherited traditions of rivalry, of memories of past wars and of the whole atmosphere of national rivalries, conquests and counter-conquests. And although the common people in almost every country want only to be left alone, they also have inherited the traditions left by old wars and conquests. As a result their governments find it comparatively easy to rouse their fears and their dislikes against other nations.

That tradition plays a large part in national rivalries is proved by the example of countries which have not inherited ancient emnities. Canada and the United States have lived side by side without wars for two hundred years. International wars are rare in South America, whatever other problems may exist there. The Scandinavian nations leave one another alone.

✠

When considering how to avoid terrorism, wars and violence, however, we must avoid the too facile method of the unilateral disarmament of our own country. To claim that Britain should disarm to set an example to the world is not to work for the cause of peace. Rather would it encourage predatory governments to take advantage of our weakness to embark on more aggressive policies.

It would appear, therefore, that crusades against war, violence and terrorism must be on an international basis, unconnected with any government, and appealing directly to the common people in every country, who desire only peace and quiet. Moreover such an appeal must not be traceable to any nation. A British, American, Russian or Chinese peace campaign is immediately neutralized by the accusations of other governments that the whole movement is 'concealed imperialism' by the nation concerned.

As many, in fact most, governments would prohibit the activities of such a crusade within their own frontiers, the movement would need to disseminate its programmes almost entirely over the air, perhaps from ships outside territorial waters. In order as far as possible to avoid the charge of being directed against any government or nation, it would necessarily at first be obliged to make use of wide objectives, such as the sanctity of human life.

This is essentially a religious theme, but need not be limited to Christianity. All who believe in God as the Creator of the world should be susceptible to the plea that only God has the right to deprive his creatures of life. When speaking in the languages of avowedly atheistic governments the theme could be slightly modified to one of pity for the victims of violence. This would not be an abandonment of principle. The objective is to draw all men to live at peace. In such a cause, we may well be all things to all men, that we may at least save some.

The wonderful discoveries of modern science too often result principally in new and more destructive methods of killing people. Let us for once use the latest scientific methods of broadcasting and of every other available scientific device to spread to the world the doctrine of the sanctity of human life. It is a change of the mental and spiritual atmosphere which we seek to introduce. This cannot be achieved by compulsion but only by positive leadership, directing human thinking into new channels.

✠

So much for the rising tide of savagery and terrorism. But the human race today is threatened not only by terrorism but by extermination. The ceaseless activity of scientists is month by month and year by year producing more and more devices for the extermination of life on earth. Rightly or wrongly, it is alleged that both the U.S.A. and Soviet Russia each have individually sufficient stockpiled nuclear and chemical devices to exterminate life on earth. If both were to use their weapons at the same time, life on our planet would be quickly extinguished.

The effect of nuclear and chemical or biological weapons cannot be localized. Even if Russia and the United States were to aim their weapons solely at one another, the nuclear fall-out, the poisons or the diseases which would result would spread all over the world. It cannot be sufficiently emphasized that, although we may not be more savage than our ancestors, the scientific methods now discovered can rapidly exterminate the human race.

Yet our ways of thought have remained entirely unaffected. Our minds still work along the old channels of national rivalries, wars, intrigues and the jealous spread of our influence in other continents. Living on a powder mine, we spend our energies playing with fire. The terrifying factor in this deadly race for death is that it is all so quiet and normal. We are solely occupied with superficialities, entertainment, sport, more money, less work and the endless musical chairs of party politics, votes and patronage.

The persons who are preparing the extinction of life on earth are respectable middle-class officials, who attend their offices or their laboratories every day and quite possibly go to church on Sundays. Soldiers who have seen the carnage of war, the panic-stricken flight of women and children, and areas of the earth reduced to wilderness and heaps of charred ruins may imagine to some degree what nuclear war may mean. But the respectable and middle-class persons who can exterminate the human race may have no such conception. They are preparing for a push-button war in which the victims of their inventions will be exterminated many thousand miles away. It is easy to imagine what could occur in a sudden confrontation. Government servants would feel bound to do their duty. Their sense of obligation to their country would prevent them from backing out in the last few minutes. In any case, such defection would be of no value when the die was cast.

Once again, the attempt to avert the extinction of life on earth must be on a worldwide scale. Pacifists who attempt to persuade soldiers to desert the service or street demonstrations against nuclear weapons are useless. A worldwide international peace movement broadcast to the world without any national or governmental affliliation would seem to be the only way to open the eyes of all the peoples on earth.

✠

We do not appreciate in the United States, Britain or Europe, that the aspects of our culture to which we are most devoted are founded on a belief in God, who has given us Free Will to enable us to make our own moral choices. Secondly, the belief that every human being has a soul which can be indwelt by God himself leads to the principle that all human life is sacred. Abandon these two principles—freedom of moral choices and the sanctity of human life—and the human race cannot survive.

There is imminent danger that the place of God will be taken by the state, to which human beings become mere pawns to be used or exterminated at will. Men would possess no more value than rats to be destroyed or enslaved as the state sees fit.

Sincere agnostics and humanists proclaim that men can save themselves by science or education, without religious belief. My immediate response is that these trends have been increasing for seventy or a hundred years, until now we are faced with a continual escalation of savagery, violence, totalitarianism and the possible extinction of life on earth. If man were able to save himself would he not be able to show at least some indications of improvement in a hundred years, instead of an ever accelerating descent to chaos.

✠

For Christians at least the issue is clear. God is a vast Spirit which created and permeates the world and can also dwell in human souls. To love God and our neighbours is our sole duty on earth. To enable us to grow into moral personalities, God has given us Free Will. To ensure that everyone has freedom of moral choice is an essential basis of Christianity. Human life is given us by God and only he has the right to take it away. The sanctity of human life must inevitably be an essential part of Christian belief.

Epilogue

The amazing and beautiful characteristics of the physical world would, I think, alone be enough to convince me that it had been created and was still being directed by an all-seeing and all-controlling Director. The principal argument, which has convinced me, however, is based on the peculiarities of the human race. The human resemblances to animals are obvious enough, but the essential differences between men and animals seem to me even more amazing. I cannot see how the qualities shown by human beings can have resulted from the automatic evolution of animals, without the intervention of any outside authority.

The following are some of the factors which convince me that men are not just animals. Firstly, all men believe in right and wrong, and all sometimes feel guilty at their own shortcomings. Man is able to stand aside and examine his own moral conduct. It does not appear that animals analyse the moral quality of their actions, but it is obvious that such a faculty would be essential to assist human beings to achieve moral progress. I accordingly believe that a sense of right and wrong has been implanted in human beings by God to enable them to rise in moral status. If God did not exist, the survival of the fittest could not have produced the moral world or a sense of right and wrong. To replace animality by morality requires a prolonged struggle, but this struggle is itself the means to achieve moral advance. If we are to become moral personalities, it must be by our own efforts.

To enable us to grow in moral qualities as individual

personalities, God has given us Free Will—the power to choose between good and evil. For Free Will to be genuine, we must have the power to choose evil. Some people will do so and will inflict harm and suffering on their fellow mortals. We blame God for the state of the world, but if he acted to prevent any of us doing wrong, he would thereby inevitably deprive us of our Free Will and reduce us to puppets.

Actions which we perform under compulsion possess no moral value. Moral progress can only be achieved if we perform good actions of our own volition. Consequently God never uses force. But if men were allowed to drift without guidance, they might all return to an animal state. To avoid such a danger, God, I believe, uses an amazingly subtle system. He can convey ideas to our minds, suggesting what course we should follow. But we cannot be certain whence these ideas come and thus we do not lose our Free Will. We can assist this guidance by asking God to show us what to do and listening for his answer. But even so we cannot be *sure* that the idea we get is from him, and thus we have to make our choice of courses and our Free Will is preserved. I find the subtlety of this plan amazing.

We complain endlessly of the state of the world, yet it is interesting to think how we would improve it if we had the power to do so. It is surprising to find that we have difficulty in thinking of any improvements which we could introduce!

In order that our right choices should lead to our moral progress, they must be based on conscientious reasons alone. If we knew for certain that rewards and punishments would be meted out to us after death, our conduct here would be influenced by personal motives. In order to maintain the purity of our motives it is essential for us to be kept in ignorance.

In guiding us to a higher moral status, God was not

restricted to the secret insertion of ideas in our minds. He is an impalpable Spirit permeating the world, utterly different from us. The example of the life of a perfect man would provide a model for human lives. To make this example effective, it was essential for Christ to be a man, 'in all things tempted as we are'.

One of the greatest lessons which he came to teach was that God is Spirit and that he can dwell in human beings. He himself seems to have been a man, but entirely saturated with the Spirit, which imparted to him a perfect moral character. I see no difficulty whatever in believing that Jesus was both God and man.

Intellectually and physically, he learned like other people. At his baptism, he received an intense spiritual experience. Retiring alone into a deserted area to think this out, he realized that neither politics nor compulsion could win over the human race, but only selfless service on the part of teachers and leaders.

He accordingly embarked on his ministry in Galilee inspired by the theme of selfless service. He emphasized the necessity of complete self-surrender to the divine service, and promised that in return God would come and dwell in the soul of the man or woman concerned. He denounced covetousness, the desire to increase our possessions, the canker of our modern civilization.

Perhaps he had hoped that the splendour of his message—that God was a loving Father who would live in us and guide us—would convert all mankind. But after two years, he began to realize that men were too cowardly to give themselves *entirely* to God. He consequently made a retreat on the slopes of Mount Hermon to re-assess his mission. Here he reached the conclusion that his task could only be completed by his own suffering and death. He made up his mind to go to Jerusalem to die.

At the last supper, Christ instituted the sacred meal of bread and wine as a memorial of himself. He also gave a staggering example of humility by washing the feet of his own disciples. He pointed the moral by saying that he was behaving like a servant.

The agony in Gethsemane is yet another proof that Christ was a man subject to the same fears as we are. Yet the indwelling Spirit soon reasserted itself, and he passed through the most intense humilations and agonies in calm serenity.

I have no doubt whatever of the resurrection. It is the only way to account for the sudden transformation of his terrified apostles into fearless heroes and martyrs.

Before he disappears from the earth, Christ promised the Spirit of God to his followers. It came at Pentecost, and still continues to do so. He had said that both the Father and the Spirit, as well as he, Jesus himself, would dwell in human beings. Our puny minds cannot understand these mysteries, but we may I think assume that God himself will live in us.

For nearly two thousand years, Christians have known the indwelling Spirit by experience, though we cannot define it in human language. Something within us welcomes the indwelling Spirit. The Spirit bears witness with our spirit that we are the sons of God. To use a crude physical analogy, we may compare the Spirit to the atmosphere, which permeates the whole world and at the same time fills our lungs.

So much for what appear to me to be the principal features of the life of Christ. In addition, he gave a great deal of detailed teaching. The beatitudes are perhaps the most famous summary of his teaching. The principal feature in this outline sketch is selfless dedication in an atmosphere of quietness and serenity. These characteristics are supported by absolutely fearless courage, able to rejoice in the face of persecution and martyrdom.

The early Church referred to Christianity as *The Way*; that is to say that it was a way of life, not a list of statements to be believed. The modern world seems to have lost the ideal of a life spent in loving, helping and saving other people. Christ 'fulfilled' the law by pointing out that mere abstention from crime is not enough. Acts of violence originate in thoughts. The only hope is therefore the interior purification of our souls. We must love our enemies even while they are ill-using us. It is impossible for those who follow Christ to advocate the use of violence in politics. Our Lord again and again denounced—by example, precept and parable—the two cankers which are destroying our civilization—greed for money and violence. He forbade us to lay up treasure on earth (Matthew 6.19), he himself owned nothing and emphasized how difficult it was for the rich to be saved. He firmly resisted all attempts to make him lead a rebellion against the Romans and told men not to resist evil (Matthew 5.39), but to accept persecution with joy.

The seventh chapter of Matthew begins, 'Judge not that ye be not judged.' Few of us pay the slightest respect to this forceful prohibition. In this age of endless talking and writing, we spend much of our time in savage or spiteful criticism of everyone else, whether they be the neighbours next door, the prominent persons in our own country or the other nations of the world. Within our own country, the misuse of the word 'equality' produces an endless flood of jealousy and resentment. Without modesty and a sense of our duty to society, our civilization cannot survive.

Christ's well-known command to turn the other cheek does not countenance cowardice. We must stand up fearlessly to the violent, but to hit back merely leads to an endless escalation of violence, which never results in a solution. Nothing happens in this life without the consent of God. Every human relationship is three-cornered, between God, the other person and ourselves. If we are surrendered to God, we can meet every situation calmly and fearlessly. Often by these means, we find a real solution.

It is impossible to imagine human life without suffering. To those who accept their suffering from God, it can become a joyful vocation.

Prayer is conversation with God, not asking him for material benefits. At home, we may try to secure quiet times at intervals during the day to read, pray and think. If, however, the Spirit really dwells in us, we should try to remember and speak to him all the day long.

Church services are an occasion to join our brothers and sisters in thanking, praising and worshipping God. The service will not be dull if we remember that God is there and we address ourselves all the time to him, in unison with our friends. Slight differences in the form of the service should not hamper us in speaking to God. All places of worship should welcome all Christians, without any differentiation between denominations.

Love, Joy and Peace are the outward and visible symptoms of the Christian way of life.

Dedication to God is an individual decision which everyone must take personally. Every soul must retain its God-given freedom of choice. Christianity is thus unable to conform to totalitarian mass movements in which the Party Line supercedes God. All totalitarian systems, whether Communist or Nazi, inevitably persecute Christians. In the modern world, Christianity is the bulwark of human freedom.

God's action is not limited to Christians. Every noble idea since the world began has been inspired. Men are so narrow-minded that they tend to cling to their local revelation and vehemently to reject all others. The best way to behave to those who profess other religions or sects, is to co-operate with them in good works, not to tell them that their beliefs are wrong. The surest way to make converts is so to live our lives that others will come to us and ask us our secret.

Christ never denounced soldiers, but sometimes praised them. As long as terrorists, criminals and aggressor nations persist, it will be necessary to restrain them by force though without hatred. Soldiers lead hard lives, which should be dedicated to the service of God and mankind.

The world at this moment is torn by terrorism and violence, and the human race is threatened with extinction by total war. In this mad bedlam of hate and destruction, it is the duty of every Christian to work and speak for universal peace, beyond individual nations or interests. But such efforts must be worldwide and practical. Petty pacifism, such as urging soldiers to desert the service, does more harm than good.

✠

God is love—that is to say that he regards all his creation with benevolence. We are his agents in this world. If we act in a spirit contrary to the will of our Creator we merely create chaos. Therefore we must forget our own selfish desires, and loyally carry out our Master's benevolent policy. This is our purpose for living.

A Short List of Books for Further Reading

Anonymous, *The Cloud of Unknowing and Other Works*. Penguin Classics.

Basset, Elizabeth, *Love is my Meaning*. Darton, Longman & Todd.

Bennett, Dennis J., *Nine o'clock in the Morning*. Coverdale House, Eastbourne.

Blackwell, Basil, *The Witness of Edith Barfoot*. Blackwell, Oxford.

Bloom, Anthony, *God and Man*. Darton, Longman & Todd.

—, *Living Prayer*. Darton, Longman & Todd.

—, *Meditations on a Theme*. Mowbrays, Oxford.

—, *School of Prayer*. Darton, Longman & Todd.

Bloom, Anthony, and Georges Lefebvre, *Courage to Pray*. Darton, Longman & Todd.

Bossuet, J. B., *Letters of Spiritual Direction*. Mowbrays, Oxford.

Butterfield, Herbert, *Christianity and History*. Collins (Fontana).

Carothers, Merlin, *Answers to Praise*. Logos International, Plainfield, N.J.

—, *Bringing Heaven to Hell*. Coverdale House, Eastbourne.

—, *Power in Praise*. Coverdale House, Eastbourne.

—, *Praise Works*. Logos International, Plainfield, N.J.

—, *Prison to Praise*. Hodder & Stoughton.

Carretto, Carlo, *Letters from the Desert*. Darton, Longman & Todd.

Caussade, J. P. de, *Self-Abandonment to Divine Providence*. Penguin.

—, *The Spiritual Letters of Father de Caussade*, Burns & Oates.

Chapman, Don John (Abbot of Downside), *Spiritual Letters*. Sheed & Ward.

Christian, An Unknown, *How to Lead the Victorious Life*. Zondervan, Grand Rapids, Michigan.

—, *The Kneeling Christian*. Zondervan, Grand Rapids, Michigan.

Coggan, Donald, *Convictions*. Hodder & Stoughton.

Crisogono de Jesus, *Life of St John of the Cross*. Longman.

Cropper, Margaret, *Life of Evelyn Underhill*. Longman.

D'Arcy, M. C., *The Mind and Heart of Love*. Collins (Fontana).

Dempster, G. F., *Finding Men for Christ*. Hodder & Stoughton.

Dodd, C. H., *The Authority of the Bible*. Collins (Fontana).

—, *The Founder of Christianity*. Collins (Fontana).

—, *The Meaning of Paul for Today*. Allen & Unwin.

Drummond, Henry, *The Greatest Thing in the World*. Hodder & Stoughton.

Eyring, Dr Henry, *The Faith of a Scientist*. Bookcraft Inc., Salt Lake City, Utah.

Farrer, Austin, *Love Almighty and Ills Unlimited*. Collins (Fontana).

—, *Saving Belief*. Hodder & Stoughton.

French, R. M., *The Way of a Pilgrim*. SPCK.

Glubb, J. B., *The Way of Love*. Hodder & Stoughton.

Goudge, Elizabeth, *A Book of Comfort*. Collins (Fontana).

—, *Saint Francis of Assisi*. Hodder & Stoughton.

Gray, A. Herbert, *Love: The One Solution*. Rich & Cowan.

Grou, Jean-Nicolas, *How to Pray*. James Clarke.

Hamilton, Elizabeth (ed.), *Servants of Love: Teresa of Avila and the Spiritual Life*. Darton, Longman & Todd.

Hilton, Walter, *The Ladder of Perfection*. Penguin Classics.

Howden, J. Russell, *Life Indeed*. Pickering & Inglis.

Hügel, Friedrich von, *Selected Writings*. Collins (Fontana).

Inge, W. R., *The Gate of Life*. Longman.

Joad, C. E. M., *The Recovery of Belief*. Faber.

Jones, E. Stanley, *Christ and Human Suffering*. Hodder & Stoughton.
—, *The Christ of the Mount*. Hodder & Stoughton.

Julian of Norwich, *Revelations of Divine Love*. Penguin.

Kempis, Thomas à, *The Imitation of Christ*. Collins (Fontana).

Law, William, *A Serious Call to a Devout and Holy Life*. Dent (Everyman's Library).
—, *Sublime Studies*.

Lawrence, Brother, *The Practice of the Presence of God*. Mowbrays, Oxford.

Lewis, C. S., *The Problem of Pain*. Collins (Fontana).

Maritain, Jacques, *Approaches to God*. Allen & Unwin.
—, *Christianity and Democracy*. Geoffrey Bles.
—, *Freedom in the Modern World*. Sheed & Ward.
—, *The Twilight of Civilization*. Sheed & Ward.

Merton, Thomas, *Life and Holiness*. Geoffrey Chapman.
—, *Seeds of Contemplation*. Burns & Oates.
—, *The Power and Meaning of Love*. Sheldon Press.

Morison, Frank, *Who Moved the Stone?* Faber.

Neil, William, *The Life and Teaching of Jesus*. Hodder & Stoughton.

Phillips, J. B., *God our Contemporary*. Hodder & Stoughton.
—, *Good News*. Geoffrey Bles.
—, *Making Men Whole*. Collins (Fontana).
—, *New Testament Christianity*. Hodder & Stoughton.
—, *Ring of Truth*. Hodder & Stoughton.
—, *Your God is too Small*. Epworth Press.

Quoist, Michel, *Meet Christ and Live*. Gill & Macmillan, Dublin.

Richard of St Victor, *Selected Writings* (tr. Clare Kirchberger). Faber.

Rolle, Richard, *The Fire of Love*. Penguin.

Ruysbroeck, Jan van, *The Adornment of the Spiritual Marriage*. John M. Watkins, London.

Sayers, Dorothy, L., *A Matter of Eternity* (Selections by R. K. Sprague). Mowbrays, Oxford.

Schryvers, Joseph, *The Gift of Oneself*. Longman.

Sheen, Fulton J., *Life is Worth Living*. Peter Davies.
—, *Way to Inner Peace*. Fawcett, Greenwich, Connecticut.

Steuart, R. H. J., *The Mystical Doctrine of St John of the Cross*. Sheed & Ward.

Temple, William, *Christian Faith and Life*. SCM Press.
—, *Readings in St John's Gospel*. Macmillan.

Teresa, St (of Avila), *The Interior Castle*. Sands/Sheed & Ward.
—, *Life of St Teresa by Herself*. Burns & Oates/Sheed & Ward.
—, *The Way of Perfection*. Burns & Oates/Sheed & Ward.

Underhill, Evelyn, *Abba*. Longman.
—, *An Anthology of the Love of God*. Mowbrays, Oxford.
—, *Concerning the Inner Life: The House of the Soul*. Methuen.
—, *The Essentials of Mysticism*. E. P. Dutton, New York.
—, *The Fruits of the Spirit*. Longman.
—, *The Golden Sequence*. Methuen.
—, *The Letters of Evelyn Underhill*. Longman.
—, *The Life of the Spirit and the Life of Today*. Methuen.
—, *Light of Christ*. Longman.
—, *The Mount of Purification*. Longman.
—, *The Mystery of Sacrifice*. Longman.
—, *Mysticism*. Longman.
—, *The Mystic Way*. Longman.
—, *Mystics of the Church*. James Clarke/Schocken, New York.
—, *The School of Charity*. Longman.
—, *Worship*. Longman.

Urquhart, Colin, *When the Spirit Comes*. Hodder & Stoughton.

Waddell, Helen, *The Desert Fathers*. Collins (Fontana).

Weatherhead, Leslie, *Discipleship*. SCM Press.
—, *Jesus and Ourselves*. Epworth Press.
—, *The Resurrection and the Life*. Epworth Press.
—, *The Significance of Silence*. Epworth Press.
—, *The Transforming Friendship*. Epworth Press.

Weil, Simone, *Waiting on God*. Routledge & Kegan Paul/Collins (Fontana).

Whelan, Joseph P., *The Spiritual Doctrine of Friedrich von Hügel*. Collins.

—, *The Spirituality of Friedrich von Hügel*. Paulist-Newman.

Wilkerson, David, *The Cross and the Switchblade*. Marshall, Morgan & Scott.